Historic Farm Buildings

AN INTRODUCTION & GUIDE
In Association with  The National Trust

Jeremy Lake

Foreword by Susan Denyer

BLANDFORD

First published in the UK 1989 by **Blandford Press**,
An imprint of Cassell, Artillery House, Artillery Row, London SW1P 1RT

Distributed in the United States by
Sterling Publishing Co, Inc,
2 Park Avenue, New York, NY 10016

Distributed in Australia by
Capricorn Link (Australia) Pty Ltd
PO Box 665, Lane Cove, NSW 2066

British Library Cataloguing in Publication Data

Lake, Jeremy
    Farm buildings of England and Wales
    1. England. Agricultural industries.
    Farms. Buildings to 1987
    I. Title
    631.2'0942

    ISBN 0-7137-1969-9

Typeset by Fakenham Photosetting Ltd, Fakenham, Norfolk.

Printed and bound in the UK by Mackays of Chatham PLC, Letchworth.

Contents

Foreword

IN the Yorkshire Dales as recently as forty years ago, many of the 800-odd field barns in Swaledale were still in use, and the rest, for the most part, were in good repair. Hay cut from the small meadows surrounding each barn was stored in the lofts and fed to cattle overwintered in the byres below. Today almost all the barns are abandoned. Many are neglected, and in the valley bottom the remarkably complex landscape pattern of small fields interspersed with barns – roughly one barn for two fields – is a landscape under threat, posing a conservation problem of staggering proportions. The barns of Swaledale, like so many others elsewhere in the country, have fallen victim to the changing fortunes of agriculture over the last generation.

The last forty years have seen an agricultural revolution of considerable scale and effort in the English countryside. The abandonment of traditional forms of agricultural labour, with their emphasis on horsepower and manpower, has been accompanied by an almost total mechanisation of farm work. No-one, least of all the farmers, could have foreseen the changes that have taken place, brought about by fundamental shifts in the economics and technology of food production, of motive power and of rural domestic life. These changes have touched almost every aspect of most working farmers' lives, and have left their indelible mark on the total man-made rural landscape, especially in the lowlands.

One of the most conspicuous effects of this agricultural revolution is the almost complete obsolescence and abandonment of traditional farm buildings. Without a use, many farm buildings have disappeared through neglect; many more are now still standing, but threatened by continuing lack of maintenance. There are no systematic figures to monitor the rate of loss of old farm buildings, but even casual observation suggests that it is considerable. The need to record this diminishing legacy and quantify the picture of general decay is now widely recognised; indeed, its execution has taken on a sense of urgency, many bodies – both official and private – responding to the challenge.

The Vernacular Architecture Group has been recording both houses and farm buildings for many years. More recently, a specialised society called the Historic Farm Buildings Group was formed to draw attention to the plight of many farm buildings, as well as to promote their research and study. The recent re-listing surveys, carried out by the Department of the Environment, have given statutory protection to many farm buildings previously not even documented, while over the last three years a countrywide survey organised by the Society for the Protection of Ancient Buildings has recorded the form and condition of some 8,000 barns.

The largest private owner of farm buildings in England and Wales, with many hundreds of farms under its protection, is the National Trust. Five years ago, as an aid to management, it embarked on a complete survey of all its vernacular buildings. When completed, the survey will have measured, photographed and described some 18,000 buildings, and the corpus of work which finally emerges will comprise a Domesday-like record of surviving agricultural buildings on National Trust land in the 1980s.

What many of these surveys are capturing is much more than an analytical record of bricks and mortar. They are looking at and recording buildings which, seen with the benefit of historical perspective, are not just a combination of materials, structure and plan, but rather built reflections of regional ways of life. In many parts of the country, farm buildings are of types that were once commonplace and plentiful; many were built from local materials using traditional techniques, and were constructed by conservative craftsmen whose methods reflected long-standing traditions. While some were structures which had evolved over the centuries to suit precisely the changing social and economic conditions of their owners and users, others were initiated by wealthy landlords and built to reflect new agricultural theories. Studies of all these buildings can bring sharply into focus the strong interplay between a farmer's life and his environment, and throw light on how such lives were lived and how they helped to shape the landscape.

It has long been acknowledged that an understanding of written history is essential for a full appreciation of all elements of the built landscape, and that for buildings to be satisfactorily understood, they should be placed in their historical context. Today, however, there is a growing realisation that buildings can be regarded as historical documents in their own right, and that there can equally well be a flow of knowledge in the reverse direction, with studies of buildings, and farm buildings in particular, contributing to our knowledge of landscape history. Moreover, such studies can produce an insight into the lives and work of people for whom the written record is largely silent, and for whom farm buildings are perhaps their only memorial. This history is not just the study of the actions and interactions of landlords, squires and monks, but also the study of the cumulative effect of the actions of many unknown, and individually unimportant people who collectively helped to shape the landscape of Britain.

Jeremy Lake's book is an introduction to the study of farm buildings in England and Wales, looked at in this way. The book will be a most useful handbook to all those who want to begin to study farm buildings as written documents, whilst also providing a foretaste of what will eventually emerge from the National Trust's regional surveys. It also adds a most worthwhile piece to the still select, but fast-growing, body of printed literature on the study of our rural agricultural heritage.

SUSAN DENYER

Preface and Acknowledgements

OUR surviving farm buildings embody the experiences of generations of farmers, from the first settlers to scientific agriculture. They manifest a wide social range, from rich man's toy to poor man's burden, and they reflect the great variety of geological conditions and farming systems of our country, from the small hill farm which required few buildings to the large arable farms of lowland areas. This book, initiated and encouraged by the National Trust, aims to explain English and Welsh farm buildings in their historical and environmental settings and act as an introduction to the subject. Readers who wish to take the subject further will find more comprehensive bibliographies and surveys of building types in the excellent works of Brunskill, Harvey, Peters, William and Weller cited in the bibliography. An Historic Farm Buildings Group, who at the time of going to press have issued their first annual periodical, have just been formed.

It is impossible to do justice to such a vast subject in such a small book, and many discoveries and topics, such as the fascinating variation of dialect terms relating to farm buildings, have had to be omitted.

I have travelled many miles to re-search material for this book, but without the kind help and hospitality of others it would not have been possible. Firstly, I would like to thank the farmers who permitted me to look at their

buildings. The National Trust provided me with much of the help I needed to start this project. I would particularly like to thank Julian Gibbs and Belinda Cousens who permitted me to quote from my surveys of buildings in the Mercia Region, Susan Denyer of the North West Region for similar reasons and for information on the Patterdale corn-drying kiln, and Jonathan Marsden for showing me some interesting sites in North Wales. I am also indebted to Isabel Richardson in Devon, Jenny and Veronica Chesher, Val Mossopp and Vaughan Upsell in Cornwall, Paul Yarker in Bransdale, Yorkshire, and Gillian McLoughlin in Northumberland, Susanna Wade Martins and Alan Carter in Norfolk, Sue and Stuart Wrathmell in Yorkshire, and John Brushe in Northamptonshire for their kind help and information on various sites; Nick Doggett guided me to the remarkable barn at Pentre'gaer Henblas in Shropshire. The documentary information on Swalcliffe is extracted from the Victoria County History for that county; Michael Bullen provided me with the references to Leighton Park and Judy Walker kindly provided information on Shugborough Park Farm.

John Steane, Susanna Wade Martins and Roy Brigden read through the book and I am most thankful to them, especially to John Steane, for their comments: I am also grateful to Chris, Angela, Judy and my parents for their support and helpful remarks on the text.

Finally, I would like to dedicate this book to the memory of my two late aunts, Dorothy and Gladys, a source of much inspiration.

1
The Rural Setting

Until well into the nineteenth century British society was predominantly rural. Agriculture employed half of the workforce in 1750, and one hundred years later it still employed one-fifth – twice the number of those in industry. Farming also provided an essential source of income for the families of industrial workers such as the tin miners of Cornwall, lead miners of Derbyshire and weavers of the West Riding.

The sights and smells of the farmyard were daily experiences for the inhabitants of pre-industrial Britain. The country parson needed farmbuildings to serve his glebe land; many manor houses, such as Packwood House in Warwickshire or Little Moreton Hall in Cheshire, were placed next to their working farms. The outer courts of medieval great houses often served as both main entry and farmyard, a feature later termed the 'base court' and common into the eighteenth century. Many English country towns were provided with barns and farmbuildings and well into this century became seething masses of farm animals on market days: the inhabitants of the salt town of Nantwich in Cheshire, the second town in the county after Chester, owned and tilled land in the fields, accommodating pigs and other animals in their backyards and built barns in the town to store hay and corn. Even the slums of the nineteenth-century industrial towns were crowded with pigsties, stables, hen roosts, cramped with cowhouses and stinking slaughterhouses.

The design and layout of farm buildings reflects the great variety of landscape and geology found in the British Isles. Agrarian techniques varied greatly within small areas, but farming practices can be broadly divided between highland and lowland zones. Corn production was concentrated in the lowlands of England to the south and west of the limestone belt, which roughly extends from Lyme Regis in Dorset to Thirsk in Yorkshire, but also in isolated highland pockets such as the Vale of Glamorgan and the coastal plain of Northumberland and Durham. In these areas, old farmsteads were large and mostly built around courtyards with large barns. The more infertile and acidic soils of wetter highland climates did not usually provide a good bite of grass for dairy cattle or well-drained soils for corn growing, and so these areas became characterised by small pastoral farms which grew small subsistence quantities of corn, grazed sheep and reared cattle for export to the fattening grounds of the Midlands and elsewhere: farms and barns were small and small ranges of farm buildings were often attached to farmhouses.

The Pattern of Settlement

Communal farming, where resources were pooled together for the common good, had been found in all areas since at least the ninth century. The open-field system, which was suited to and most common in the more densely populated arable lowlands of southern and central England, was based upon two or three large fields which encircled the village; these fields were divided into strips which were distributed amongst the villagers, whose farm-steads lay on one-quarter to one-half acre (1–2,000 sq m) plots (called tofts) in the village. A remarkably preserved example of such a village can be seen at Laxton in Nottinghamshire. Villagers in open-field parishes were initially the tenants of manorial lords, and paid cus-tomary rents and dues: they also, however, sat on village councils which nurtured and regulated communal farming through 'common consent'. Common grazing, fodder, fuel and building materials could be found out-side the bounds of these fields – on wood pasture, meadow, fenland, moorland or heath. Fertility was en-sured by rotating crops, folding animals on land after harvest and preventing over-intensive cultivation by leaving one field uncultivated (fallow) each year.

The strips of open fields were sepa-rated by earth banks, not hedges, and contrasted with the fields of anciently enclosed areas, divided by trees and hedges, described by John Worlidge in *Husbandry*, 1694: 'the Hedges are all re-plete with Timber and other Trees, that they are deservedly called The Wood-lands and were so called in former Ages'. Woodland areas, often found intermixed with the nucleated villages of open-field parishes, are still charac-terised by a dispersed settlement pattern; examples are the Forest of Arden in Warwickshire and the Weald of Kent and Sussex. In these areas farmsteads of ancient date were cleared by free and independent farmers. For example, Antioch Farm was founded in Dorset's Vale of Blackmoor in 1244 and Luck-ings Farm, in the Buckinghamshire Chilterns, was founded in the early 1300s by Richard de Lovekin of Coleshill.

Domesday Book (1086) already made a clear distinction between the large open-field villages of lowland areas and the ancient pattern of enclosed and isolated pastoral farmsteads mostly found amongst the hills and valleys of highland areas. Many farmsteads around Penwith and on the Lizard peninsula in Cornwall lie amongst Bronze and Iron Age field systems. The Devon landscape of steep hills and small valleys which encouraged small en-closed family farms had been completed by about 1300 and in northern England many farmsteads were founded by Scandinavian settlers – in the Lake Dis-trict, for example, Watendlath origin-ated in the tenth century as a Norse settlement meaning 'end of the lake', and a Viking 'thing' mound remains at Fell Foot Farm, Little Langdale.

In the north and west, therefore, set-tlement remained dispersed and the hamlet of three to five families formed the ideal settlement type. Highland far-mers usually practised the infield-outfield system, whereby the infield near the farm was constantly cropped and manured and the outfield was set aside for rough grazing and occasional-ly ploughed up for corn. In Wales, English-style open-field villages are only found dotted along the Anglicised main river valleys, the fertile Vale of Glamorgan and the north coast, and in

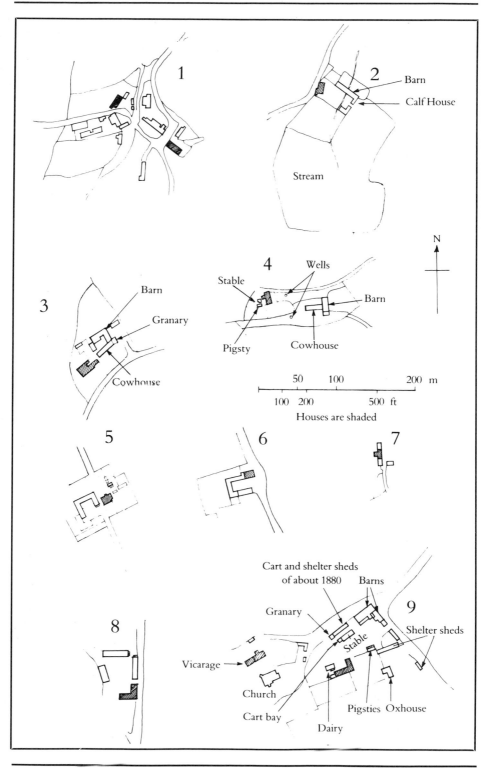

1

2 — Barn
— Calf House

Stream

N

3

Barn

Granary

Cowhouse

4 Wells
Stable
Barn
Pigsty Cowhouse

50   100   200 m

100 200   500 ft

Houses are shaded

5

6

7

8

Cart and shelter sheds
of about 1880 Barns

Granary

9

Shelter sheds

Vicarage

Stable

Church

Cart bay

Dairy

Pigsties Oxhouse

south-west England along the coast and river valleys.

Transhumance, the seasonal movement of livestock to fresh pastures, remained a vital pasture right in these upland areas. All the folk of Devon, for example, had the right of grazing their cattle upon Dartmoor in summer, and in Wales and northern England cattle and sheep were also taken up to high ground in summer, leaving hay to grow in the meadows. In Wales the permanent valley settlement was known as a 'hendre' and the summer house as a 'hafod'. In ancient Welsh laws summer houses ('hafotai') were described as temporary structures made of forked branches with wattle and turf walls; in the 1770s, Thomas Pennant described them as one-storey buildings with stone seats and haybeds ranged along the walls. Women there made butter and cheese, and the men tended the herds and the harvest, although it is important to add that many summer houses were little more than an hour's walk from the permanent homestead. Population pressure, especially in the sixteenth century, led to the expansion of farmsteads onto high marginal land not suited for

1. Farm layouts varied according to topography, farming regions, social status and period of building. In highland areas, houses on smaller farms (below 100 acres), were attached to their buildings in linear (7) or L-plan (fig. 36) layouts, but larger farms would have their buildings detached (4) or built around yards (8). Hamlets with dispersed layouts of houses and buildings (1) were most common in western Britain. Farmsteads with dispersed layouts were often the result of gradual growth (9). The courtyard farm (5 and 6) was common from the late eighteenth century on large lowland (over 200 acre) arable farms which had been improved or enclosed.

(1) *Frogwell, Cornwall.* Dispersed layout of houses and early nineteenth-century farm buildings.

(2) *Trevarda Farm, Llansallos Bay, Cornwall.* Late eighteenth-century buildings: the steam powered the water wheel in the barn, rushed through the tentering yard (for hanging cloth), and finally flushed the privy.

(3) *Lye Hall, Dudmaston, Shropshire.* Fifteenth-century house, L-shaped barn dating from late seventeenth century, and cowhouse and granary of about 1800.

(4) *Brithdir Mawr, Cilcain, Flintshire.* House dated 1597, early seventeenth-century barn, stable and pigsties. Late eighteenth-century cowhouse attached to barn.

(5) *Gallows Hill, Wallington estate, Northumberland.* The buildings date from about 1822 when the eighteenth-century one-storey farmhouse was rebuilt: to the north of the house lie pigsties and a holding pen for sheep.

(6) *Prior Hall, Wallington estate, Northumberland.* Farmhouse dated 1784, three-door cowhouse dated 1777 to south, barn and byre to the west, and granary above shelter sheds and stable to north.

(7) *Seventeenth-century linear farmstead.* From Ysbyty Ifan, Caernarvonshire, showing house flanked by cowhouses.

(8) *Low Hall, Appletreewick, Yorkshire.* Farm buildings built around yard in about 1691.

(9) *Cogges Manor Farm, Witney, Oxfordshire.* A manorial site, with the house dating from about 1242, the barns from about 1680 and 1700, the dairy from the medieval period, the granary and oxhouse from the eighteenth century, the shelter sheds from about 1800, pigsties about 1840 and cart and shelter sheds to north from about 1880. The stables were converted from a small barn in about 1700 when the large barns were built.

2. *Dunnabridge Pound Farm, Dartmoor, Devon*

The seventeenth-century farmhouse and two cowhouses adjoin a large circular pound, one of those whence cattle pastured on Dartmoor were driven four times a year. At these annual 'drifts', the tenants of Dunnabridge watered and pastured the impounded cattle in return for a 'halfpenny loaf'. Similar pounds were used in open-field villages to hold foreign animals which had strayed on to common land: an early nineteenth-century example can be seen at Swaffham Prior in Cambridgeshire.

keeping cattle in winter: by the early nineteenth century, sheep grazings had replaced all but a few of the last '*hafotai*'. Summer settlements in northern England were known as 'shielings', which were groups of stone huts and corn drying kilns. Population pressure since the medieval period had prompted the building of permanent farmsteads on old shielings, but in the sixteenth century the process accelerated and many of the last summer houses were abandoned after Union with Scotland in 1703. Many of these former shielings retain the word 'shield'. For example, Lynnshield Farm south of Haltwhistle in Northumberland has a small seventeenth-century house – probably dating from its creation as a permanent farmstead – which was converted into a granary in about 1800 when the existing farmhouse, byres and barn were built.

The Foundations of Husbandry

Before improvements in communications, especially railways from the 1830s, both highland and lowland regions – however specialised – needed a broad mix of farming systems. 'An housebande [farmer] cannot thrive well by his corn without he have cattell, or by his cattell without corn' pronounced Fitzherbert in his *Boke of Husbandrye*, 1523. Corn provided grain and straw for animal fodder, thatch and daily bread, and cattle and sheep provided hides, wool, meat, tallow, milk, cheese, and essential manure for fertilising fields of corn and other crops; sheep and corn husbandry; whereby sheep droppings fertilised growing fields of corn, was an essential feature of most large arable farms, and the ancient Welsh Gwentian Code referred to the importance of 'yard dung'. The annual corn harvest was, in the words of W. G. Hoskins, 'the most fundamental fact of economic life – a source of plenty or a harbinger of famine.'

The higher the ground, the shorter the growing season, but even in Wales, half of which is 180 m (600 ft) above sea level with an annual growing season of only 240 days, subsistence quantities of corn had to be grown and oats (which unlike wheat could grow in damp climates) remained a staple crop. Walter Davies wrote in 1810 that 'On some parts of the Hiraethog Hills in Denbighshire, no grain is sown but the hardy oat', and much the same may have been said of the Pennines, Peak District, Cheviots, Cumbrian mountains, Dartmoor and other upland regions where small corn barns bear witness to poor productivity. By the seventeenth century the hill farmers of the north and west mainly specialised in dairying and cattle breeding and drove their cattle along the droving roads to the fattening grounds of the south and east. In southern and eastern Wales and lowland England, especially East Anglia, the drier climate permitted the growing of great quantities of grain – barley and especially wheat – which were stored in large barns.

James Caird, in 1851, estimated that three acres (1.2 hectares) would be necessary to provide adequate supplies of winter hay for one cow. This obviously restricted the numbers of cattle that could be kept over winter, but certainly autumn did not see the wholesale slaughter of livestock: even a thirteenth-century Gloucester Abbey Cartulary only exhorted that 'no useless and unfertile animals are to be wintered on hay and forage'.

However, the balance between livestock and corn, or 'horn and corn', was precarious and could easily be upset by pressure of population upon limited resources. Over 90 per cent of land being farmed in 1914 was under plough or hoof as early as 1086, and by 1347 population had increased from 2.5 to 5.6 million, which forced much reclamation from woodlands and marginal upland soils: in the Derbyshire Peak District, for example, the outlines of arable fields can still be seen over 1000 ft above sea level at Tideswell and Weston. The yield of corn from the land was so low (a ratio of crop yield to seed sown of about 4:1 compared to the present norm of 40:1) that arable land had to encroach upon available pasture, livestock numbers declined, and as less manure to fertilise the land became available farmers were locked in a vicious downward spiral which, combined with worsening weather, culminated in a series of disastrous harvests in six out of seven seasons between 1314 and 1321 and cattle plague between 1319 and 1321, resulting in terrible famine. It needed a collapse in population and more livestock to reverse this trend. After the Black Death of 1349 and subsequent epidemics, labour shortages prompted the expansion of pasture farming and the beginning of ley farming (which alternated corn and grass), leading to increases in yields. As early as the late fourteenth century, grain yields had increased most on those of the Bishop of Winchester's manors where more stock were kept.

By 1600 the ratio of crop yield to seed sown had increased to about 10:1, a yield rarely exceeded before about 1800. The invention of irrigation for water meadows in the late sixteenth century increased the value of meadows tenfold and the amount of hay produced by fourfold. From the 1630s irrigated meadows were introduced in the chalk downlands of southern England, which, combined with efficient sheep and corn husbandry, resulted in greater yields of corn. Such improvements laid the foundations for the so-called Agricultural Revolution of the eighteenth and nineteenth centuries.

New grasses, such as sainfoin, clover and trefoil after the 1640s and perennial rye grass from the 1670s were used to cultivate artificial meadows. Farmers in Norfolk, under Dutch influence, had been the first to use new artificial grasses and root crops in a new four-to-six year rotation of crops which alternated between wheat, turnips, barley and clover; in the 1640s Sir Richard Weston was the first to plant clover seed under a nurse crop of corn. Turnips, being a leafy smother crop, kept weeds to a minimum and if they were planted in rows regular hoeing (especially horse hoeing) removed other weeds. Such a system was practised by Colonel Walpole of Houghton in Norfolk as early as 1673. Moreover, these root crops and new grasses restored fertility to tired land by fixing more nitrogen into the soil and livestock, especially sheep, would be folded

upon turnip fields and thereby fertilise the ground with their manure. On heavier soils turnips would be pulled out of the ground and fed to cattle in farm yards; the manure was then taken back to the fields and thereby helped to increase yields. Turnip husbandry had been accepted in most parts of the country by the 1750s, although upland areas continued to rely on hay for winter fodder into the nineteenth century. In the Dwyryd valley, Wales, hay barns with slate pillars still survive as products of nineteenth-century drainage.

The other major improvement was made possible by the continued expansion of large farms and enclosed fields: unlike open fields, enclosed fields were easy to manage and convenient for experimentation with new techniques, and they did not harbour disease because they were not overstocked. Even in the thirteenth century village councils could not prevent wealthier peasants from snubbing rule by 'common consent' and, by exchanging strips in the open fields, creating their own enclosed fields. Indeed, 45 per cent of woodland and open-field England was enclosed by 1500. In the eighteenth and early nineteenth centuries much moorland and the remaining open-field parishes of England (a further 24 per cent) were enclosed by successive Acts of Parliament, and most village-based farmsteads were re-sited out in the fields.

Improved techniques therefore laid the basis of agricultural prosperity, and not until the 1850s did a general labour shortage prompt the introduction of machinery on a grand scale: for example, the Bell's and McCormick's reapers, invented in 1826 and 1812, were not used until after the 1851 Great Exhibition. Our surviving farm buildings illustrate the variety and ultimate development of farming methods, and the functions of these buildings will be the subject of the next chapter.

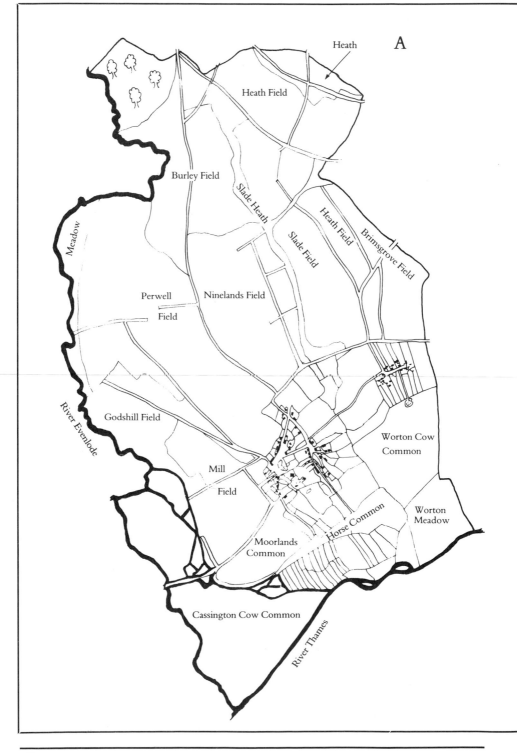

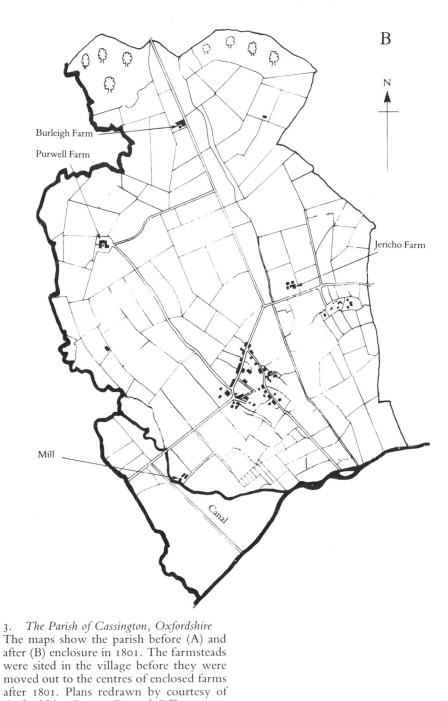

B

N

Burleigh Farm

Purwell Farm

Jericho Farm

Mill

Canal

3. *The Parish of Cassington, Oxfordshire*
The maps show the parish before (A) and
after (B) enclosure in 1801. The farmsteads
were sited in the village before they were
moved out to the centres of enclosed farms
after 1801. Plans redrawn by courtesy of
Oxfordshire County Record Office.

2
Buildings for the Farm

Barns

THE largest building in most farmyards was the barn, which was mainly used to store and process the fruits of the annual corn harvest, to provide straw and chaff for animals, and set the scene for the harvest home supper when the last waggon load of corn was brought to the yard amid much rejoicing. Paul Hentzner, travelling near Windsor in 1598, 'happened to meet some country people celebrating their harvest home: their last load of corn they crown with flowers, having beside an image richly dressed, by which perhaps they would signify Ceres. This they keep moving about, while men and women, man and maidservants, riding through the streets in the cart, shout as loud as they can until they arrive at the barn'.

The barn entrance needed to be large enough to admit a loaded waggon and was often given a large porch which protected any incoming load from inclement weather. In more pastoral upland areas, far smaller carts or even sledges were used, and such porches were rarely built. Once inside, the sheaves of corn were unloaded into the outer bays of the barn. In Shropshire

and Suffolk horses were brought into the storage bays to tread down the corn as it was being unloaded, the distraught animal finally being lowered down by a rope slung across one of the roof beams.

To prevent the crop becoming mouldy or overheating, ventilation was essential. Hence the ventilation holes or slits found in stone and brick barns, with much variety of pattern: triangular openings formed of stone slates found around Stonesfield in Oxfordshire, the elaborate patterns such as lozenges found in brick barns of the north and west Midlands, or the open wattle panels of timber barns, notably those along the Welsh Borders. Stone barns often have square ventilation holes, originally the 'putlog holes' used for scaffolding (see fig 20). 'Owl holes' situated high in the gable ends allowed access to owls which killed any unwelcome rodents.

Over the winter months, the barn echoed to the sounds of flails beating grain out of sheaves of corn. This method, known as threshing, had been in use for at least 2,000 years, and processed not only corn but also beans, clover seeds and other crops. The work was physically demanding and unhealthy, for besides the risk of cracking one's head with the flail, one inhaled great quantities of dust: to Walter Rose, the thresher could be distinguished from other agricultural workers by his pale complexion and to Lord Ernle it was 'the most unwholesome of rural occupations'. Extra workers would be recruited from the farm on very wet or cold days. The monotony was relieved by working in groups and by timing the flail-beats to create different rhythms – such as simulating the clanging of church bells.

Threshing floors needed to be very clean (the threshers often wore slippers) and were often made of one-inch thick oak planks: these are mostly found in the two-storey barns of Cumbria, parts of Wales and the south-west, where barns were often built over animal houses (see fig. 46). Threshing floors could also be made of brick, earth or clay, of stone flags or cobbles. In Glamorgan, the sheaves were threshed on projecting kerbstones flanking the threshing floor.

Threshing floors were usually sited in the centre of barns, in the through-entry, but it was also common to site the threshing floor to one side of the barn: this last arrangement left a small bay to one side of the floor for the stor-

4. *Threshing c. 1900* The flail was made of two pieces of wood linked by a universal joint: this enabled the thresher to grip firmly the handle (usually of ash) and, using a circular motion, bring the beater (usually of holly or thorn) down onto the ears of corn. Photograph courtesy of the Mansell Collection.

5. *Barn of c. 1800 at Lynn Shield, North-umberland, and early seventeenth-century barn at Pentre'gaer Henblas, near Oswestry, Shropshire (right)*

The usual position for the threshing floor was in the centre of the barn. Many barns, as at Lynn Shield, had their threshing floors placed towards one end, most bays storing corn and the single bay receiving threshed straw: such barns were particularly common in upland areas which grew only oats and were also associated with the introduction of threshing machines (pp. 105–7) from the 1780s. Barns could also house animals (see fig. 46). The seventeenth-century barn at Pentre'gaer Henblas has a central cart entry flanked by haylofts above cowhouses, which retained timber-framed partitions housing 24 cattle. The raised oak-planked threshing floor is entered by the steps to the right; further to the right is storage for corn.

age of threshed straw, often with access to a cowhouse. Low partitions often separated threshing floor from storage bays (see fig. 4): in the stone regions of northern England and Wales these were made of slate slabs, but in timber areas, notably in the north and west Midlands, timber-framed partitions separated the unthreshed from the threshed corn; in other stone regions, planks of wood often sufficed for such partitions and have therefore left no trace. Planks were often slotted into the bottom of the doorway to prevent hens wandering in and corn flying out during threshing: an enclosed space or 'corn hole' for the storage of threshed grain can sometimes be found next to the threshing floor.

Another way of storing corn, known from the sixteenth century, was in ricks, which were stacked in a walled yard just outside the barn. With the introduction of machine threshing from

the late eighteenth century the crop was processed much more quickly and therefore rickyards became larger: many new barns were built with the threshing bay to one side, and mostly stored straw (see p. 106).

After threshing, the corn was winnowed by using the draught created by the opposing open barn doors to separate the grain from the dust and chaff: the heaviest (and best) grains were thrown furthest, the light 'tailings' which fell nearest the thresher's feet being fed to the animals. Barns in hill country often have a small 'winnowing door' opposite the main entry, but some barns do not have opposed doors, implying that winnowing was performed outside, as in warmer Mediterranean climes: winnowing stands, called 'plats' or 'platts', occur in Cornwall, parts of Devon and south Wales. A good draught could be arti-

ficially made by revolving a drum with sheets nailed to it. Winnowing fans, included in some fourteenth-century inventories of monastic granges, and winnowing sheets were also used.

Barns were not only used to store corn and other crops, for ample evidence from inventories shows that they also stored hay. Barns in all areas had room set aside for cowhouses and stables (figs. 5 and 46), and the small doorways found in many barns indicate that when empty in spring they were used for other purposes such as sorting livestock and shearing.

Threshing was made much easier if corn was first dried, so loosening the grain from the husk. Drying kilns were mentioned in Anglo-Saxon and ancient Welsh laws, have been excavated on medieval sites throughout the country, and remained in use on hill farms in wetter parts of the country. In simple

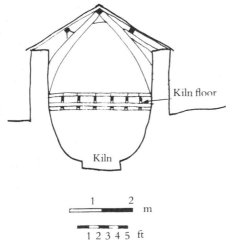

Kiln floor

Kiln

1   2 m

1 2 3 4 5 ft

6. *Corn-drying kiln, Ullswater, Cumbria*
This is sixteenth or early seventeenth century, and a rare survival of a once-common building type. The building is built into a slope and has a kiln beneath a drying floor made of slates. Photograph courtesy of The National Trust/Tim Whittaker.

kilns, the corn was placed on a straw or horse-hair cloth and laid over crossed lengths of wood above the kiln, which consisted of a fire burning in a hole dug out of the ground: in some areas the cloth could be unrolled in front of the house fire. Corn-drying kilns can still be found in farmhouses in Somerset, Devon and Dorset.

Cartsheds and Granaries

Threshed grain and implements could be stored in the farmhouse, but the owners of large cereal-producing farms needed separate storage buildings. The ploughs, harrows, carts and other implements of arable husbandry were stored in the cartshed, which usually faced north because, in the words of Gervase Markham, 'The Sun does more harm to a cart than either Wind or Rain'. They are still known as 'cart-shades' in Northumbria. Cartsheds, mentioned in medieval documents, were open-fronted buildings with walls to the sides and rear: cartsheds with openings to front and rear were rare for, although they made unhitching easier, implements could not be stored against the back wall.

Freestanding granaries were built in the corn-growing south and east of England from at least the fifteenth century, and in more pastoral areas such as Devon and the Welsh borders from the seventeenth century. Granaries were needed not only to store corn for sale but also held corn for seed or fodder. They needed to be out of reach of vermin, especially rats, and to be well ventilated and have their walls sealed against infestation by insects. Therefore they were raised on mushroom-shaped staddle stones, had removable steps, and the floors inside were made of seasoned and fitted planks; plastered walls and tile or slate rather than thatch roofs kept bugs away; grain was packed in sacks or stored loose in wooden grain bins, and granaries were ventilated by louvred windows, in order to prevent mould and germination.

Granary doors often had cat holes enabling the farm cat to catch rodents and were also fitted with locks – not against strangers, but the farm's own carters. 'Carters of the old school would sooner starve themselves than their teams' wrote Thomas Hennell, and 'to fetch more corn from the granary when the farmer was away was not looked upon as theft' wrote Walter Rose. It was commonplace for the granary to be

7. *Granary, Ipsden, Oxfordshire* Note the mushroom-shaped saddle stones, whose overhangs defeat rats. Walls are usually of timber frame with either brick infill or clad with weatherboard, tile or slate. Freestanding granaries like this were mainly built in the south and east of England, others occurring in the south-west and along the Welsh borders. This granary is mid-eighteenth century, and adjoins the largest barn in Oxfordshire (see p. 91). Photograph courtesy of Oxfordshire Museum Services.

built next to the house, the farmer keeping the key to the granary himself, but the tales are still legion of how carters would carefully pull out the staple of the lock or drill holes in the floor replacing them with knotted wood to disguise their pilfering.

These raised granaries were clearly descended from the helm (also known as the hovel and hemble), described in Midland court rolls from the fourteenth century as a structure which placed the corn stack on a rough timber floor raised above the ground by low walls or staddle stones.

8. *Granary over a cartshed, Downs Farm, Barrett Ringstead, Norfolk* A popular type of farm building. This one is eighteenth century and served a large arable farm. Sacks of grain could be carried up outside steps which give access to a gable-end door or hoisted through a trapdoor in the cartshed floor. Photograph courtesy of Norfolk Historic Farm Buildings Survey.

Other hovels had corn and bean stacks raised above open-fronted sheds for animals or carts. Fitzherbert, in 1534, and Thomas Tusser, in 1557, recommended such buildings. Marshall recorded the storage of bean stacks in this way in the open-field parishes of northern and central England. Davies described the use of such 'hembles' in north Wales in 1810, and Bailey and Culley noted in 1805 that Northumbrian farms had outbuildings with corn stacks over cartsheds or shelters for yearling cattle. Tusser mentioned that hovel roofs (which could also store brushwood and other fuel) could be placed on 'Crotchets' (forked posts), and this simple construction enabled them to be moved about the farm. These types of hovel evolved to become in permanent form the granary over the stable or cartshed, a popular type of farm building which survives from the sixteenth century.

Stables for Horse and Oxen

Oxen and horses powered the ploughs and other machinery used on the farm. The traditional eight-ox plough team could plough an acre in a day, and remained in use into the 1900s in Yorkshire, the Cotswolds, Devon and Cornwall, Somerset, Herefordshire and South Wales. The oxherd of the eleventh century *Rectitudines* had to 'fill the stalls of the oxen with hay and water and carry out their litter' and a boy goaded on the oxen 'hoarse from cold and shouting'. Over 1,000 years later, Thomas Hennell recalled that 'The oxman had three or four songs, which he sang continually over and over again; and when he stopped singing, the oxen stood still in their tracks'.

Horses needed a more varied diet than oxen, regular shoeing (oxen were only shod for road transport), and constant care to prevent them from falling ill. Moreover, oxen, unlike horses, did not lose their value after retirement because they could be fattened up for meat and were also blessed with a quieter temperament. However, the invention of the horse collar in the eighth century enabled the horse to perform twice the work of an ox. From at least the thirteenth century horses were used with oxen in mixed plough teams and on their own for lighter tasks such as harrowing; from the seventeenth century the revolution in farming methods led

9. *The Oxhouse, Manor Farm, Cogges, Oxfordshire* Very few identifiable oxhouses have survived. This building, which is probably eighteenth century, is detached from the farmyard and has eight stalls with stone water troughs. Oxen were used on many farms in this area in the nineteenth century. It now houses Dairy Shorthorn cattle.

10. *Working horse stables, Manor Farm, Cogges, Oxfordshire* This stable housed six horses, tethered to iron rings on the manger. Other stables had stalls, stoutly built to withstand kicks and with raised fronts to prevent horses from biting each other. Stables also had boarded bins for holding chaff and corn bins or 'arks' for bran and oats. A floor of pitched stone aided mucking out. The typical stable door, with its detachable upper half, and the half-glazed window with sliding ventilators (popular from the 1830s) provided light and ventilation. The door to the right gives access to the riding horse stable shown in fig. 11. Courtesy of Oxfordshire Museum Services and John Steane.

to an increase in lighter work such as harrowing and pulling two-horse ploughs not suited for oxen. At Speke Hall in Lancashire twenty draught oxen and five work horses worked the estate in 1524, but by 1700 the 'Draught Horse Stable' had become the sole power-house of the farm. The introduction of horse-driven threshing machines, harrows, rollers, reapers and other machines, especially from around 1800, increased demand for farm horses, and by 1911 937,000 horses worked on our farms. In some areas horses were still regarded as newcomers: thus farmers in the parish of Llanfihangel in mid-Wales addressed their cows in Welsh but distinguished their horses by giving them English names such as Prince or Captain.

Labels within illustration: Loose box for single horse · Loose box for single horse · Open stabling for two horses · Hay rack · Manger · Tethering rings · Manger · Hay rack · Harness cupboard · Harness hooks · Corn bin · Pitched stone floor · JMS

11. *Riding horse stables, Manor Farm, Cogges*
Looseboxes are known from the early
nineteenth century, serving as foaling pens,
hospitals for sick horses and stabling for riding horses which needed space in which to
stretch their legs. Courtesy of Oxfordshire
Museum Services and John Steane.

The average farm horse was ready to
work at four or five years old, would
retire at fourteen and continue to do
light work until twenty. The number of
horses per farm varied according to
farm size and topography and to the
ratio between plough teams and the
number of older horses kept on for
lighter work, but one horse to twenty
acres was an oft-quoted figure.

Stables were the hub of the working
farm, and at 5 or so in the morning the
carter's day started with mucking out,
feeding and harnessing the plough
teams, and there the farmer arrived to
bark out his orders for the day. 'Pride in
horses' was the carter's watchword, and
the stable was often the most elaborate
building on the farm.

Hay lofts, with their characteristic
circular or square pitching holes, provided insulation for horses which
sweated profusely after a hard day's
work in the fields. Hay could be pushed
from the loft into feeding racks. Agricultural writers from 1585 (Christopher
Clifford's *Schoole of Horsemanshippe*) recommended that hay racks be placed
vertically, thus preventing seeds falling
into the horses' eyes, but limited space
meant that, except on large gentry
farms, most racks were placed diag-
onally against the wall. Recesses in the
wall held medicines, grooming kits or
candles: stable candles were a frequent
item of expenditure from October to
March.

In East Anglia and Oxfordshire, horses were sometimes accommodated in shelter sheds opening onto a walled yard. The hackney or riding horse, a smarter animal which the farmer used for supervising his estates and going to market, was accommodated in a more elaborate stable with plastered ceilings. Large stables had harness rooms with fireplaces to keep the carters warm and the harness supple.

Buildings for Sheep

Sheep provided not only meat, wool and tallow but also milk and cheese (especially in the medieval period), and dung to manure arable land.

Walter of Henley, in the thirteenth century, recommended buildings for milking and lambing over winter. The ewes in Bolton Abbey's sheephouses on Malham Moor in Yorkshire produced milk and cheese, and in the sixteenth century William Camden described 'those cheese sheds which they call the "Witches"' on the pastures of Canvey in Kent. Ten milking ewes, however, were only equivalent to one cow and by the seventeenth century cow's milk was preferred.

Sheepfolds, enclosures made of wattle hurdles, were used to pen sheep in certain areas and so enabled the animals to enrich the land with their manure. Their dung was so important that the medieval lords of Norfolk ruled that their tenants' sheep had to graze on their land, and a sheet anchor of arable farming on the southern English downs was the daily round of driving sheep down from their feeding ground to be folded on the cornlands at night. A. G. Street, writing in his *Farmer's Glory* (1932) about a sheep and corn farm in Wiltshire, noted that:

It always seemed to me that the farm was run entirely for the sheep and most of the men were jealous of the shepherd's conse-

quent importance. One of my father's labourers frankly hated sheep. 'We be either lambing 'em, runnin' 'em, marken 'em, shearing 'em, dipping 'em, or some other foolishness. And they can have all the grub we do grow, and God knows how much it do cost the Guvnor for cake.'

Buildings for sheep were therefore temporary structures and not at all reflective of their past importance. On most farms a lambing house could be converted from any cowhouse or shed: in 1851 James Caird noted that South Downs sheep about to lamb were kept only in roughly thatched sheds of wattle hurdles. The great sheep shearings of spring time, the most important communal event after harvest, were often performed in barns. Crostenrigs Barn, Troutbeck, built for Benjamin Browne in 1733, had a cowhouse, calfhouse and stable, the latter adapted for use by sheep. In the Yorkshire Dales and especially in the Lake District, one-year-old sheep (called hoggs) spent their first winter in hogg houses: these are small buildings with low 1.5 to 1 m (5 ft to 3 ft 4 in) ceilings and rough lofts for hay above, and their ruins are dotted around many fellsides (see fig. 46). William Marshall found similar buildings in late eighteenth century Herefordshire but very few have survived. Older sheep, especially in the Cheviot Hills, found shelter and hay in round sheep stells which were so shaped to prevent the harbouring of snow drifts.

Sheep, being constant nibblers, also need constant moving about to prevent overuse of pasture. Wheeled cabins, where shepherds slept and kept medicines, were illustrated in medieval manuscripts and became a common sight on English downlands. Sheep could spend the whole summer on lusher coastal grazings and one can still see the nineteenth-century brick shepherds' huts on Romney Marsh in Kent where sheep were brought to fatten in the summer.

Cowhouses and the Supply of Fodder

Cowhouses (also known as byres and shippons) have been documented since prehistory, but despite their widespread use on large estates they did not become popular until after the 1780s. Cows are more susceptible to disease when housed at close quarters indoors but are more productive and need less food. William Cobbett, in *Cottage Economy*, 1821, said that a cow left out would have half the yield of one housed indoors over winter. Another reason for housing was that the hooves of wandering cattle would damage winter pastures (especially those on clay soils) and most importantly, manure from housed cattle could be easily collected and distributed over arable fields. In many areas, such as Norfolk and Pembrokeshire in the early 1600s, cattle had previously manured the land by being folded upon it within hurdle enclosures, like sheep.

In contrast to the stable, the humble cowhouse had a lower and wider door, rougher beams and a sweeter meadow smell. Cows needed a good water supply, provided by the farmyard pond (see fig. 42) or a standpump; ventilation was poorly provided in early cowhouses but in the nineteenth century large windows with adjustable sliding ventilators were introduced. Cows were either tied to stakes, used since the medieval period in parts of Wales or the south-west, or were restrained in their stalls by wooden clamps.

Loose boxes were used from the eighteenth century to house sick animals or bulls, and mainly young and fattening cattle. Ranges of looseboxes on a farm imply cattle breeding or fattening. In north-east Wales, for example, a recent survey found that they were mostly concentrated in the Clwydian Hills, where calves from the sur-

12a. *Cowhouse interior, Merionethshire* Cattle were usually stalled in pairs and separated by partitions of oak or slate. Note the hayracks and that the floor slopes to a drainage gutter behind. Mangers for roots became increasingly common after the 1780s. Photograph courtesy of the Institute of Agricultural History and Museum of English Rural Life, University of Reading.

12b. *Cowhouse at Wenalth Farm, Talgwern, near Machynlleth, Monmouthshire (left)* Cowhouses such as this are common in highland regions. In lowland areas and on improved farmsteads built from the eighteenth century (see Chapter 7) shelter sheds and foldyards are more common (see figs. 42, 49, 54). Photograph courtesy of the Institute of Agricultural History and Museum of English Rural Life, University of Reading.

13. *Loosebox, Okehampton, Devon* Looseboxes for calves were not mucked out as
frequently as cowhouses and were often
provided with a step down to a lower floor.
Calves installed in autumn consequently
rose up on a tide of straw and manure, and
often were difficult to extricate in the fol-
lowing spring. See also fig. 56. Photograph
courtesy of the Institute of Agricultural History and Museum of English Rural Life,
University of Reading.

rounding dairy areas were brought in
to fatten. A rare and more expensive
form was the hammel, which had a
walled yard for exercise in front of a
loosebox.

Cattle could also be accommodated
in open-fronted shelter sheds opening
onto yards (see fig. 42), which by the
eighteenth century were used for fatstock and young cattle; straw from the
barn was liberally spread over the yard
floor for use as bedding and to absorb
dung. Eventually, the soaked and

heavy mixture would be forked into muck carts and then spread over fields ploughed for corn. As a result, these shelter sheds are mainly found in developed lowland areas which had large farms with plenty of workers, had plenty of corn for straw, specialised in raising cattle for beef rather than dairying and used the manure to fertilise large acreages of arable land. In pastoral areas with small family farms and little corn for straw, cattle were stalled in cowhouses and often bedded without straw, being given the straw to eat, and produced liquid manure which was easier to dispose of: a characteristic feature of upland cowhouses are muck holes used for shovelling out manure. In hill country, bracken was harvested both as fodder and as bedding, and holly, heather and gorse were cut for fodder: gorse had to be specially crushed before feeding. In 1596, Leonard Mascall recorded that woodland farmers short of hay or straw gave their cattle oak, elm and ash leaves.

The production of hay for these animals was an essential part of grassland management. Hay could be stacked outside in ricks but was better protected if kept under cover in lofts or barns. Timber-framed hay barns, built on saddle stones, had open panels for ventilation; brick hay barns, especially those late eighteenth- and nineteenth-century examples from Cheshire and the West Midlands, were built with many decorative openwork panels. True Dutch barns (fig. 46) with adjustable roofs set on posts set in the ground

14. *Barn at Oak House Farm, Hampstead Norris, Berkshire* Barns of this type were common in southern England, and were used for the storage of hay or threshed straw. Eighteenth- and early nineteenth-century writers noted many timber-framed barns of this type around London, which stored hay for the capital's horses. Photograph courtesy of the Institute of Agricultural History and Museum of English Rural Life, University of Reading.

15. *Dairy at Cogges Manor Farm, Witney, Oxfordshire*
Note the settling pan for separating cream from milk, the barrel churn for butter-making and the cheese press. The word 'DAIRY' printed over the outer door originates in a decree of 1795 that dairies should be exempt from window tax.

which could be moved up and down by a jack-winch, were depicted in paintings from the fifteenth century and were once popular in Britain: Walter Davies, for example, noted their use in North Wales in 1810. In Cornwall, they were known as mow-hays and had wood posts or even posts of great stone slabs, as at The Leaze on Bodmin Moor. More common were haybarns with fixed roofs: North Merioneth has many fine slate and stone examples. The iron-framed hay barn (now known as Dutch barns) became popular after the 1880s, especially after many cowhouses with low ceilings and hay lofts had been replaced by spacious one-storey buildings open to the roof.

Dairies and Pigs

The dairy could be either a detached building or attached to the house. It needed a good water supply: the yard outside the dairy at Cogges Manor Farm Museum in Oxfordshire has a well and a covered pentice for drying out washed utensils. The dairy also needed to be cool and well ventilated, and so it was invariably situated north of the house, protected by trees and partly sunk into the ground, with cool flagstones on the floor, whitewashed walls and cross-ventilation provided by shuttered windows without glazing. The dairy provided plenty of space and shelving for butter and cheese-making; shallow pans were needed for separating the cream from the milk, earthenware pots for the cream, plunger churns or barrel churns with handles for turning the butter, and cheese vats and cheese presses. On some farms, water wheels powered dairy churns: a fine dairy farm at Plas Glasgwym near Betws-y-Coed has a dairy

powered by water wheel, the stream finally rushing past a range of pigsties. In south-west England the famous clotted cream was made by separating the cream over a fire, with no use for churns. The watery skimmed milk or whey was traditionally fed to pigs, pigsties often being found associated with dairies. On some large Victorian farmsteads, they are connected by brick whey pits.

Gervase Markham in *Cheap and Good Husbandry*, 1614, knew the pig as 'the husbandman's best scavenger and the huswife's most wholesome sink'. The annually slaughtered pig was of great importance to the rural masses; the peasant Piers Plowman, creation of the fourteenth-century poet William Langland, had 'his beard beslobbered with bacon' and Flora Thompson's *Lark Rise to Candleford* recalls the pig's importance to Oxfordshire villagers of the 1890s.

At autumn, pigs were fed on the nut crop known as mast; Markham said pigs could be fed on mast for up to eight weeks, being left to root about

16.   *The Pigsty* The shelter can accommodate two pigs or a sow and her litter, and is entered from a small walled yard, for food, water and exercise; some yards had water and food troughs which could be filled from outside by a chute, which made feeding much easier. The picture shows a Black Berkshire pig, once popular but now a rare breed.

the woods under the supervision of a swineherd, and there are references in his time to herds of pigs being driven many miles to feed in woods at autumn; but the crop was unreliable and Leonard Mascall's *Book of Cattel*, 1596, recommended that it be harvested and mixed with hogwash for housed pigs. Indeed, Markham himself noted that pigsties were more common in open field areas (where woods were scarce) than in woodland areas. By the 1800s pig swill was heated up in the brewhouse or back kitchen. On Welsh farms, the detached brewhouse was known as '*y gegin foch*' (the pigs' kitchen).

Pigs could be fattened in yards but the usual type of shelter was the pigsty, either roughly made or the characteristic tiled shelter with or without a yard in front. At Church Farm, Sandiacre, Derbyshire, the pigs were housed in caves hewn out of the rock and several examples elsewhere, especially in southwest England, have pigsties built into walls or made of stone slabs; at The Leaze on Bodmin Moor in Cornwall remarkably primitive shelters have been made of stones and boulders gathered from the vicinity. Medieval farms, such as those owned by Battle Abbey, Sussex, had ranges of tiled piggeries. Parsonage farms in late seventeenth- and eighteenth-century Cornwall had pigsties made of earth or stone with stone slate roofs.

Dovecotes, Geese, Poultry and Bees

Doves and pigeons were another vital source of fresh meat, eggs and manure. Unlike poor man's bacon, pigeon pie was a rich man's dish, for the keeping of pigeons – along with fish and rabbits – was a manorial right restricted to parish clergy and manorial lords. This right was much resented, for a pigeon could eat its own weight in corn every day, and clearly did not discriminate between the fields of its owner and poorer neighbours. In 1811, William Gooch estimated that the average Cambridgeshire dovecote produced 1200 young pigeons each year, selling at between 2s 6d and 5s a dozen.

The distribution of dovecotes clearly reflects the former extent of manorial control and arable farming. They are still very common in the former open-field parishes of the Midlands, particularly Nottinghamshire, but are least common in areas such as north-west England where there was less corn or fewer great landowners; in Wales, dovecotes occur only in the arable and manorialised Vale of Glamorgan, Anglesey and the north coast. By the early seventeenth century, however, manorial control had weakened and laws relaxed: a contemporary estimate put the number of dovecotes at 26,000, but probably the greatest number of dovecotes were built between 1650 and 1750 when corn was cheap and relatively abundant, and an Act of 1761/2 permitted any tenant to build his own dovecote with his landlord's permission. Many farms from about 1600 had dovecotes, but more had nesting holes for doves built under the eaves or in the gable ends of farm buildings.

Dovecotes were invariably built away from the bustle of the farmyard and if gentry houses had dovecotes they were sited near the kitchen garden, for their droppings were highly valued as manure for vegetables and fruit – it was also used as a medicine.

The egg collector would use a potence, a form of revolving ladder fixed to a central pivoted post, to make the collection of eggs as easy as possible. To accommodate the potence circular dovecotes were built: this was the most common type used in the medieval period, but on account of their simple form they are very difficult to date. The square dovecote at Hill Croome, Upton upon Severn, Worcestershire, is cruck-framed (see pp. 50–53 and fig. 22) and may therefore date from the fifteenth century, and other examples of square dovecotes exist in stone, as at Bruton in

17. Dovecote at Kinwarton, Warwickshire
The ogee-headed doorway is the only clue to its fourteenth-century date. The walls are whitewashed. Note the louvred glover on the roof, which allowed the pigeons to fly in and out of the dovecote. The photograph of the interior shows the potence which facilitated easy access to the 580 nesting holes. Photographs courtesy of The National Trust/William Muirhead.

Somerset (*c.* 1580) or in timber frame as at Wichenford in Worcester (*c.* 1600). The square dovecote was less convenient, for the potence could not reach its corners, and so octagonal brick dovecotes became very popular in the eighteenth century.

In 1614, Gervase Markham wrote that pigeons 'must have their rooms and boxes made clean once a week; for they delight much in fair buildings'. Nesting holes were built in various ways. Stone dovecotes have nesting holes with perches of projecting stone courses. Timber-framed dovecotes might have nesting holes made of brick or timber frame, or mud with slate slabs or wooden pegs acting as perches: a good example of the latter type is at Toft in Cambridgeshire where the nesting holes are of clay blocks with arched openings, and cob dovecotes had nesting holes cut out with paring knives (see pp. 40–45).

No farm would have been complete without its fowl, which were left to scratch about the yard. The hen-house could be built in a loft above the pigsty, out of the way of foxes and other predators. Rows of pens might accommodate broody hens or geese. Such might be the function of the unusual early nineteenth-century Gothic-style range of pens at Great Tew, Oxfordshire, and the range at the 1863 farm at Crow Leasowes, Bitterley, Shropshire. At Baulking, Oxfordshire, there is a typical mid-nineteenth-century two-storey goose house: the geese were grazed on the village green during the day and then driven back to spend the night in the first floor of their goose house. Goose pens could be made by leaving square holes in dry-stone walls and these are found in the wet moorlands of the north and west: in Cornwall these holes are paired and known as crows (the local name for a shelter). Geese were often grazed on wet ground, because they ate the liver fluke, a deadly

pest which afflicted sheep and thrived in wet conditions.

Bees were kept for their honey, which was used to cure hams and preserve fruits, to make the ancient Celtic drink of mead (made from grain and honey) and make wax for church candles. The modern type of wood hive which had removable mesh frames for inspection and honey extraction was imported from America in the 1860s. The most ancient type of beehive was made of wickerwork daubed with clay, but from at least the seventeenth century less cumbersome hives of coiled straw (called skeps) were preferred.

These hives were placed on beestones above the ground on timber stands resembling bird tables or, more commonly, in bee boles. Bee boles, openings made in south- or east-facing stone or brick walls, were particularly common in the west and north where they protected bees from the wet climate. At Packwood House, Warwickshire, they are found built into the brick walls of the seventeenth-century kitchen garden. An alternative arrangement was to place hives on shelves in bee houses. A very fine sixteenth-century example can be seen at the Hartbury College of Agriculture, which originally came from Minchinhampton at Nailsworth in Gloucestershire and is made of Caen stone. Large 'walk-in' bee houses with passages for inspection were built from the late eighteenth century, as at Attingham Park in Shropshire, where there is a fine example of a bee house near the walled garden, with wooden latticed walls and two tiers of bee skeps.

In late spring, when the new queens were ready to hatch, about half the colony would leave the hive as a swarm with their old queen. Small hives encouraged swarming as a way of creating new colonies. 'A swarm in May is worth a load of hay' goes the old saying, and the beekeeper, having made a good supply of skeps, kept careful watch for

the earliest sign of a new swarm. At the end of the summer, bees in hives with poor and good yields were killed off and those in the medium–yield hives were left to overwinter: special buildings for winter storage had no windows and are now very rare.

18. *Dovecote at Erdigg, Clwyd* Octagonal brick dovecotes became the most popular type used in the eighteenth century. Photograph courtesy of The National Trust.

3
Materials and Builders

TRADITIONAL, or vernacular, buildings were built of many different materials reflecting the astounding variety of geology found in Britain. Until recent times, the use of such materials was conditioned by their availability and by the wealth of their builders.

The majority of writers who wrote reports to the newly founded Board of Agriculture from the 1790s noted the prevalence of what they considered to be flimsy building materials, such as mud, thatch and timber, on old-fashioned farmsteads and in areas now associated with stone or brick. When William Marshall visited Wiltshire and the Hampshire Downs in 1798 he recorded that large farmhouses were built of prestigious bricks and tiles with outbuildings of wood and thatch, but that small poorer farms were all made of 'mud and straw'.

Earth is the most ancient and widely used building material known to humankind. In East Anglia, and especially in south and central Norfolk, clay blocks were simply dried out and used for walling: such walls, set on brick plinths and with a protective coating of gas tar, date from the late eighteenth century. There are more examples of cob, an ancient type of mud walling which consists of water added to a mix of clay and dung, with chopped straw and broken slate or stones acting as binding agents. The weight of this wet mixture caused cob walls to be made thick – 0.7 m (2 ft 6 in)) is a common width – and built up in layers separated by straw. After the 1790s the use of shuttering, whereby the mixture was packed down between boards, made thinner walls possible. Once dried, the walls were trimmed down with a paring knife and given a protective coat of whitewash or thin coat of mortar.

Cob was very common, but surviving examples are now concentrated in areas like Britain's western peninsulas whose small farmers lacked good building stone or timber, or sufficient clay or fuel for making bricks. In Cornwall, George Worgan wrote in 1810 that cob was widely used before his lifetime and seventeenth-century surveys of Cornish parsonage farms record the use of mud and thatch for pigsties, cowhouses, barns and other farm buildings. In 1679, for example, the surveyor found at Botus Fleming a recently rebuilt house of stone and slate and outbuildings built of mud and thatch. Cob is still found on the Lizard Peninsula: at Rosuic, an outhouse with external stone steps, probably a granary and typical of

many farms of the south-west (fig. 46), has a thatch roof and cob walling set on a high stone plinth, whilst nearby is a range of early nineteenth-century stone and slate outbuildings, evidently of the new type admired by Worgan. The same situation prevailed in Devon (with

19. *A Devon cartshed* Many farm buildings were crudely made and, as this photograph of about 1860 clearly shows, were erected as temporary structures. Photograph courtesy of the Institute of Agricultural History and Museum of English Rural Life, University of Reading.

the probable exception of Dartmoor), where stone and slate outbuildings continued to be built in the nineteenth century with eaves, courses and gable walls made of cob.

Walter Davies, in 1810, had commented on the widespread use of cob in Wales – an earlier writer had likened the Welsh cottage to 'A great blot of cow-turd' – but cob buildings are now only found in the Lleyn and Pembroke peninsulas: a surveyor of the Faenol Estate in Lleyn noted in 1779 that most farm buildings were made of mud with

thatch roofs. No examples are now known from Cheshire, where a survey in 1773 of the Tollemache estate recorded a 'low mean old stable of mud and sticks' at Wettenhall and a 'little old mud cowhouse'. Cob and day lump can still be found in Northamptonshire, Buckinghamshire and Nottinghamshire where it was used for dovecotes and other farm buildings well into the nineteenth century.

A similar mixture built around a rough framework of earthfast timber posts was known as 'mud and stud'. Robert Lowe, an observer of Nottinghamshire's agriculture, wrote in 1798 that many poorer farm buildings were made of mud and stud, this material being also used in the coastal lands of Lancashire, Lincolnshire and Cumbria's Solway Plain – all areas where timber and fuel for making bricks were in short supply. For similar reasons mud and stud buildings were still common in the late eighteenth century open-field Felden areas of Warwickshire and Worcestershire.

Cob was easy to make and cheap, using not only unskilled labour but also locally available materials, and for this reason became popular amongst poorer farmers. Thus William Hutchinson, in his *History of Cumberland* (1794), wrote that 'These clay houses are generally made up in a day or two, for, when a person wants a house, a barn etc built, he acquaints his neighbours who all appear at the time appointed: some lay on clay; some tread it, whilst others are preparing straw to mix it with. By this means building comes low and expeditious and indeed it must be owned that they have brought the art of clay building to perfection'.

The raising of a timber frame or timber roof upon stone walls would also

20. *A north Devon farmyard, c. 1900, showing cob and thatch buildings* Without a good roof – usually of thatch – and a tall plinth of brick or stone, cob walls would disappear back into the earth whence they came. Note that the dairy on the left has a protective coat of limewash. To the right is a calfhouse and in the centre a linhay (see p. 93). The muck heap is surrounded by raised stone paving, often known as a causeway. Photograph courtesy of the Beaford Centre, Devon.

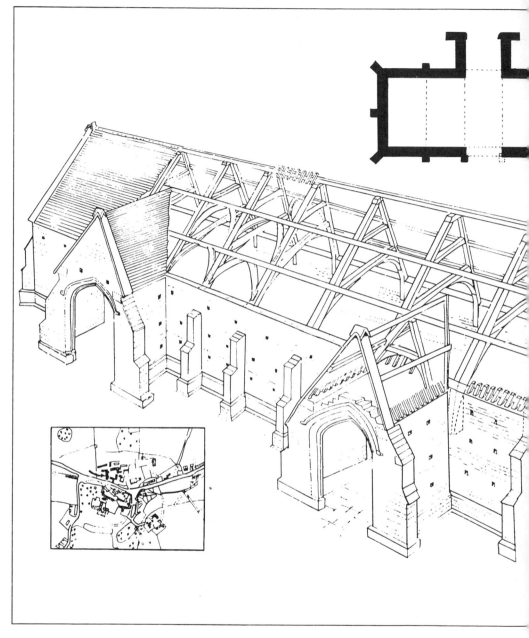

demand the help of unskilled labourers, who were duly rewarded for their efforts with gifts of beer or food. At 'le Reysing' of a barn at Ormesby, Norfolk, in 1434, 1s 2d was spent on bread, ale and cheese. In Cumbria, James Jackson of Holm Cuttram recruited 30 of his tenants to build his cruck barn in 1662, and in July 1688 Sir Daniel Fleming spent ten shillings on ale 'at ye raising of ye great barn' at Coniston. Now only traditional communities such as the Amish of Philadelphia still practise barn-raising. However, it was specialised

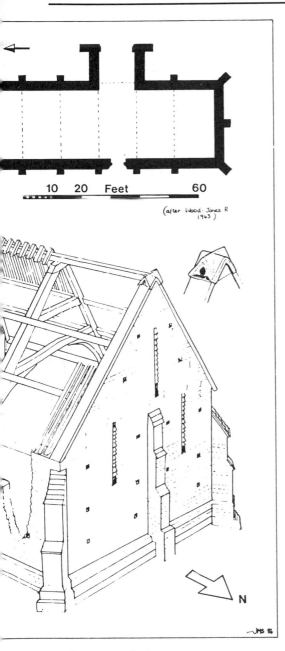

10 20 Feet 60

(after Wood-Jones R 1963)

N

—JMS 85

21. *Swalcliffe Barn, Oxfordshire, c. 1400*
Notice the put-log holes for the scaffolding
and the ten-bay raised cruck roof. Another
similar but smaller five-bay barn remains.
The other buildings included a 'Great Gate'
built by the mason John Coventry, a bake-
house, a slaughterhouse, a stable, and a
dovecote and granary all built between 1439
and 1441. The yard had an earth floor made
of earth, sand and water. Courtesy of Oxfordshire Museum Services and John
Steane.

Wykeham's new foundation at New
College in Oxford had acquired the site
in 1389; Wykeham respectively built
and rebuilt other New College barns at
Upper Heyford and Adderbury. At
Adderbury the owner of the barn was
less involved with supervising the
building operation, his main task being
to pay the masons and supply the stone,
but at Swalcliffe New College was
closely involved from the start.

In August 1399 five men, including
two '*firmarii*' or farmworkers and one of
the college bursars, were sent to Strat-
ford where they stayed for four days
supervising the selection of timber for
the roof from the wood at Bewlepark
next to Bordesley. Some of the stone
came from as far as Winchcombe in
Gloucestershire, and 61,000 stone slates
were brought from Slaughter and Norton and lime for bonding and torching
from Ascote. The warden and fellows
from New College made frequent visits
to the barn to check on progress.
Richard Wynchcombe, the Oxford
mason responsible for work at the fine
chancel of Adderbury church, worked
on the barn in 1405 and probably carved
the door mouldings of the two great
porches on the east front; Thomas
Rede, another mason who had worked
at New College and Adderbury
Church, probably carved the saddle
stones which surmount each gable. In
1404 timber from Kingham was
brought for scaffolding and the purchase of 13,000 slates in that year (fol-

craftsmen such as carpenters, masons,
tilers or slaters who were responsible
for designing and making these buildings.

A remarkable set of building accounts
survives for the building of Swalcliffe
barn in north Oxfordshire. William of

lowed by 26,000 for 1405) suggests that the work was completed in stages, with one end finished first. In 1406 iron hinges and blocks were bought for two doors which weighed 86 lb. A smaller five-bay barn flanks the north side of the yard, and examination has suggested a similar building sequence, the final stretch of walling being finished after the last cruck had been slotted into position.

Similar types of cruck roofs to the New College barns, but without arch braces and of slighter build, are known from other Oxfordshire barns at Tadmarton and Church Enstone and in other fifteenth-century buildings in the Banbury region. The Rectory Barn at Enstone still has an inscription which records that it was built in 1382 by Walter de Wynforton, Abbot of Wynchcombe, 'at the petition of Robert Mason, Bailiff of this place'.

Medieval peasant farmers, like farmers today, certainly erected some temporary shelters or cob walling on their own, but recent research has shown that they also employed carpenters to build barns and other farm buildings.

The activities of specialist craftsmen, for example, can be traced in many Lake District buildings. Early stone buildings were made from stone picked from moorland or riverbed – such as Wall End Barn, Langdale, 1612–15 (see fig. 43). Later stone buildings used watershot masonry whereby the stones were tilted so that rainwater was thrown off without penetrating the joints: a barn at Seathwaite Farm, Borrowdale, used this technique and is still inscribed with the names of its builders, G. and B. C. Banks, 1851. Benjamin Browne, of Townend Farm in Troutbeck, set out the time of completion and specifications (which included dimensions) for his builders when he wrote out his contract for the building of Lane Barn in 1730. A scale drawing was compiled by the builders, who also built Crostenrigs Barn for the Brownes and repaired Troutbeck Church.

Another contract drawn up by the Brownes in 1772 for the rebuilding of a stable at Lowood, Troutbeck, goes to extraordinary lengths to specify its dimensions and internal fittings: for example, 'In the Stable one Horse rack quite across as also a Manger: three Shell Stalls with fore posts, tail posts and sleepers to be done wether with board or stone. One step ladder up into the barn: a partition between the Stable and peat House. Three Doors with Checks and Seals . . .' and so on, 'the work to be finished before the usual time of lying in of Hay'.

Building skill was often passed down from father to son. The workshop of Walter Rose, who wrote in 1934 of his life as a country carpenter, had a beam marked 1569 – the date when his family first acquired their property. The fine old workmen of his father's workshop 'had never been separated from the land, and so they understood the ways of farms and the needs of the farmers as no town carpenter could possibly have done. They knew from long experience all there was to know about the erection of new farm buildings and repairs to the old, the making and repairing of gates and fences in the fields, of cattle cribs and sheep troughs and all that pertained to the farm'.

The carpenter, therefore, played a vital role in making farm buildings and was employed to build not only timber buildings but also the roofs and fittings for stone and other mass-walled buildings. The most essential items in the carpenter's basket, an axe or adze for trimming timbers and a selection of shell-bit augers for drilling holes, and his most basic joints, such as the mortice and tenon, had hardly changed since prehistory. However, it was probably the introduction of better iron saws in the thirteenth century that made possible improved jointing methods, especially the lap-dovetail joint which joined roof truss to wall frame and facilitated the emergence of a fully fledged tradition of timber framing. Indeed, excavations at Barton Blount in Derbyshire found that in the fourteenth century the construction of a sawpit signalled the change from earthfast mud and stud buildings to timber-framed buildings.

Timber-framed buildings were prefabricated. The timbers were assembled in a carpenter's yard, the joints marked with Roman numerals known as carpenters' marks, and were then taken apart and carried to the building site, where the marks – which were sequentially ordered – guided the carpenter as he reassembled the building. The principal load-bearing roof trusses divided buildings into 'bays', each about 4.6 m (15 ft) long and possibly based on the accommodation needed for the traditional eight-ox plough team. These bays have formed a common unit of measurement since the medieval period: for example, in the seventeenth century corn and hay in a barn at Speke Hall in Lancashire was measured by the bay or half-bay. Timber-framed barns resisted condensation and internal pressure from stored crops better than mass-walled buildings, and for this reason remained popular into the nineteenth century: a fine example dated 1854 lies south of the Berkshire Ridgeway near Ashdown House. Early brick barns (up to about 1760) often have buttressed walls or timber-framed partitions to withstand such pressure.

It might take up to twenty trees to build a three-bay timber-framed barn – mainly oak, but elm, ash and even poplar were also used. Rods of hazel or ash for making the wattle infill panels would have come from the coppiced and pollarded trees of carefully managed woods, hedgerows or wood pastures. These wattle panels were either left open for ventilation or daubed over with a mixture of clay, cow dung and even road scrapings. From the seventeenth century, brick was used as infill in some areas. Another option was weatherboard (figs. 42 and 43A) nailed horizontally onto the frame, which is mainly found on the timber-framed farm buildings of south and east England. Early weatherboards were made of oak or elm, usually about three quarters of an inch thick and rebated or overlapped over each other. In the eighteenth century, thinner and narrower boards were used to cover increasingly light frames of Scandinavian softwood which had straight rather than curved braces.

A particularly unusual form of boarded cladding is found on some early barns. The great medieval barn at Frindsbury in Kent has vertical boards slotted into the sides of closely spaced posts, evidently integral and not added later to the frame. This technique can also be found in other medieval farm buildings, such as the fifteenth-century granaries at Colville Hall, White Roding, Essex, and Tadlow, Cambridgeshire, and in seventeenth-century Shropshire barns such as at Hodnet Hall or Pentre'gaer Henblas (fig. 5).

Techniques of timber-framing and building roof trusses for mass-walled buildings varied from region to region, and showed strong differences between the traditions of highland and lowland areas. In the south and east the walls were erected first, and each roof truss was then raised into position. There was no longitudinal support because each truss was stiffened by its aisled construction with complex parallel or scissor bracing pegged across the frame. These roofs are also characterised by the uniform size, or scantling, of their roof timbers and are therefore known as common rafter roofs: the earliest of these roofs are found in the aisled medieval barns of lowland England.

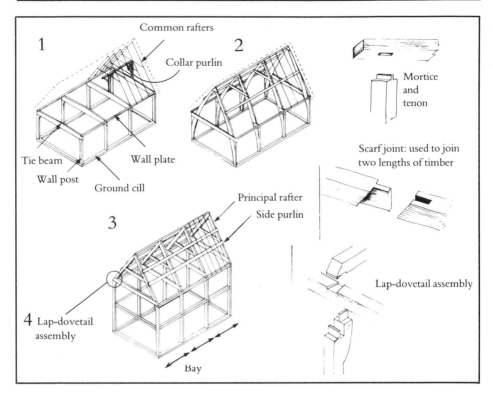

22. *Perspective views of* (1) common-rafter roof, showing collar purlin and crown post, (2) cruck barn, (3) post and pad building (after Smith, 1975), (4) lap-dovetail assembly. Courtesy of the National Monuments Record for Wales.

However, roofs needed some form of longitudinal support and for this reason purlins were introduced. Collar purlin and crown post roofs are found in the medieval to seventeenth-century aisled barns of south and east England (especially Kent and Essex) – nearest their point of origin in twelfth-century northern France. The great fourteenth-century barns at Frindsbury, Kent, and Falmer Court in east Sussex used the crown post, as also did the St Alban's Abbey estate in about 1400 at Kingsbury and St Julian barns, St Alban's, and Croxley barn, Rickmansworth. The side purlin is also first found in common rafter roofs, such as the Wheat Barn, Cressing Temple, Essex (*c.* 1250) and Great Coxwell, Oxfordshire (*c.* 1300), where they are found clasped between the collar and main rafter of each truss. (See fig. 24)

The full cruck was a very different form of roof which now has a marked highland distribution and does not occur at all in East Anglia or the southeast. The cruck roof frame was the first item to be assembled and raised into position. 'Scotch marks' on the faces of surviving crucks were used to support temporary shoring, before the ridge piece and side purlins were trenched into the backs of the cruck blades. Therefore, in contrast to common rafter roofs, the load was mainly carried by the roof frame, and not the walls: the sill beams and stone plinths of many Yorkshire cruck barns are interrupted every bay by cruck blades which rest on pad stones. However, the disadvantage of

23. *The Barley Barn, Cressing Temple, Essex* The Barley Barn of about 1200–20 and Wheat Barn of about 1275–85 at Cressing Temple stand on land owned by the Knights Templar between 1150 and their suppression in 1308. The tops of the aisle posts are not thickened: the typical thickened or jowled head (see fig. 22(4) and 45) was developed during the thirteenth century. Note the fifteenth-century crown post roof and that the bays, defined by the aisled roof trusses, create a sense of rhythm within the barn – characteristic of aisled barns. Photograph courtesy of the Royal Commission on the Historical Monuments of England.

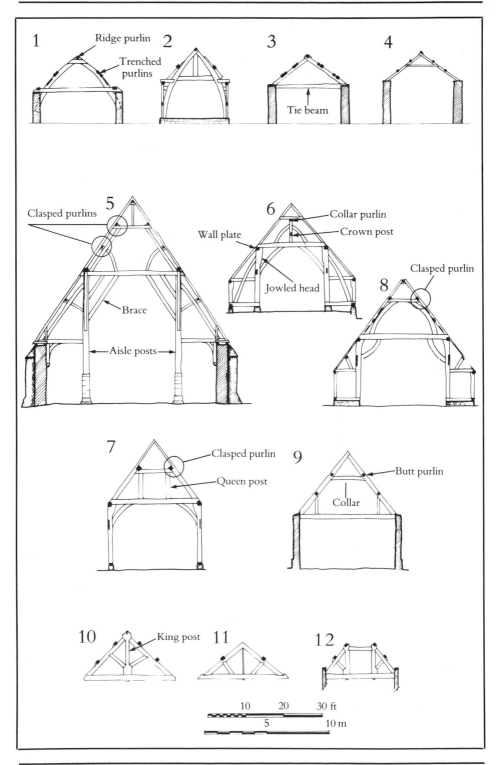

the cruck for barn construction was that its size was limited by the size of timber that could be obtained and so base crucks (see fig. 29) and raised crucks (as at Swalcliffe) were devised to get the maximum width and height. Cruck roofs were built on highland farms of the north and west until the eighteenth century but east of the limestone belt and in other prosperous areas were not built after the sixteenth century: in the West Midlands, for example, the three-bay cruck barns of peasant holdings were superseded by post and pad barns after 1500.

The post and pad building, which borrowed features from both traditions to create a fully integrated timber frame, is difficult to date because its form, once perfected, remained un-altered for centuries. Thus Walter Horn has dated Harmondsworth barn in Middlesex to the thirteenth century,

24. *Sections of Roof Trusses* Seventeenth-century cruck barns at (1) Low Hallgarth, Little Langdale, Cumbria, and (2) Stryd Lydan, Flintshire, now in Welsh Folk Museum (after Wiliam, 1981). Eighteenth-century roofs with trenched through purlins from (3) Derwentwater, Cumbria, and (4) Cotehele, Cornwall. Crown post roof from (6) fourteenth-century barn at Court Lodge, Brook, Kent (after Rigold, 1966). Roofs with clasped purlins from Oxfordshire, (5) Great Coxwell Barn, c. 1300, (7) seven-teenth-century barn in Vale of the White Horse, and (8) barn dated 1743 near Watl-ington. There is a striking similarity be-tween the ridge and purlin housing of (5) and (8). Note contrast to typical butt purlin roof from (9) barn of c. 1680 at Cogges Manor Farm, Cogges, Oxfordshire. (10) King post roof of about 1820. F. Price, in *The English Carpenter*, 1733, was the first to illustrate the standard king-post roof which became very popular on British farms: from the early 1800s they were made from im-ported softwood and secured with iron nuts and bolts (as was (12), a queen-post roof of about 1820). The king post could also be replaced by an iron post (11).

but the historians of the Victoria County History have dated it to 1426–35 – a dispute that could be settled by dendrochronological or Carbon-14 dating.

The efficiency of the post and pad roof ensured that by the late sixteenth century roofs with side purlins had emerged as a dominant type south and east of the limestone belt, although builders in the south-east retained the clasped purlin and diminished principal rafter as a keepsake of the common-rafter tradition. For example, in Ox-fordshire clasped purlins were used in the Vale of the White Horse and east of Oxford into the eighteenth century, but west of the Thames and Cherwell – on the edge of the limestone belt – butt purlins had taken their place by the seventeenth century. A similar contrast exists between the clasped purlin roofs of the Vale of York and the trenched purlin roofs of the surrounding Dales. Roofs with trenched purlins are domi-nant in highland regions and are clearly derived from the cruck tradition: the king post (fig. 45) was a particularly common roof-type in Yorkshire from the fourteenth century, as at Bolton Abbey Barn. Other areas which lay be-tween highland and lowland zones, such as Dorset and the Cotswolds, used butt purlin roofs instead of cruck or clasped purlin roofs from about 1600. In Norfolk, which was neither touched by the cruck tradition nor has a rich legacy of aisled buildings, clasped purlin roofs were superseded by butt purlin roofs after about 1580 (as at Paston Barn, dated 1581).

Beams in many farm buildings ex-hibit peg holes and mortice slots which show that they have been reused and this has given rise to the widespread belief that such beams, especially in barns, are ships' timbers, salvaged from the wrecks of boats and ships. Daniel Defoe observed in the 1720s that in coastal Norfolk 'the farmers and coun-

try people had scarce a barn, or shed, or a stable ... but what was built of old planks, beams, walls and timbers ... [from] the wrecks of old ships'. While this may certainly be true of coastal Norfolk or around the breaking yards of Kent's Medway valley, there are no buildings elsewhere made from ships' timbers. Indeed, virtually all reused timbers were salvaged from old houses or farm buildings and court records and other documents show that the reuse of materials was an active part of landlord policy from medieval times.

The use of roofing materials was also dictated by cheapness and availability. William Marshall found that farm buildings in the Kent and Sussex Weald, a densely wooded area, were roofed with oak shingles, these being the 'splinters and shavings of hoops' from local woodland industries. In upland areas of England and Wales heather from surrounding moorland was used for roofing, now replaced by slate or corrugated iron. Turf, ferns or rushes

25. *Dovecote at Hawford, Worcestershire, and Dovecote at The Old Vicarage, Tintagel, Cornwall* These two dovecotes show differences in building technique between different parts of the country. The seventeenth century Hawford dovecote is timber framed and built of substantial close-set timbers typical of the western English school of carpentry. The dovecote at Tintagel, which is probably fifteenth century, has a corbelled stone roof: such roofs were used to build Neolithic megaliths and tombs in the Mediterranean and northern France, and to build the huts of Celtic missionaries in Ireland. Farm buildings which use corbelled stone roofs are found in Brittany, southwest England and south Wales (all areas with close historical links) and comprised pigsties (especially south Wales), ash houses (Devon) and medieval dovecotes (such as Oxwich Castle and Monknash Grange, Glamorgan, and Cotehele House, Cornwall). Photograph of Hawford dovecote courtesy of The National Trust Photographic Library/Andy Williams.

were employed in other areas. Rush straw, from uplands or badly drained land, rotted very quickly; reed thatch was preferred if available, and in Norfolk it was cut on the Broads and taken up to 40 miles inland: with a ridge of wheat straw and laths of strong reeds, such a roof could last for 100 years. Wheat straw thatch was only of considerable importance in arable lowland areas: in southern England and the Vale of Glamorgan straw or reed thatch was combed and pegged or sewn down. In western Wales, wattles of hazel, alder or willow were used as underthatch, on which were placed bundles of straw thatch (often rye or barley) with a turf ridge. Bundle thatch was used in most areas and survives in some Midland counties, as at the oxhouse at Cogges Manor Farm, Witney, Oxfordshire (fig. 9): bundles of twigs placed on rough roof joists were covered with straw thatch, thereby saving the use of roof trusses.

Stone slates and clay tiles were not common before the eighteenth century except on wealthier farms. The stone slates of the medieval barn at Carlisle were held in position with pegs of sheep bones and those of Swalcliffe by iron nails; the fourteenth-century barns built for St Alban's Abbey (p. 50) had oak-pegged clay tiles. Weatherproofing could be effected by pushing moss between the slates or, from the eighteenth century, torching the underside of the slates with a mixture of lime plaster and cow hair. Pantiles, another popular roofing material (especially from the eighteenth century), were imported from the Netherlands and used in East Anglia, lowland Yorkshire and the eastern Yorkshire Dales and Moors, and made in the port of Bridgewater in Somerset whence they were exported to the coastal areas of north Somerset and Devon.

Stone slates, Welsh slates (marketed throughout the country from the late eighteenth century) and clay tiles are usually associated with farmsteads re-built during the eighteenth and nineteenth century enclosures and im-provements in brick and stone, the lat-ter comprising everything from flint and chalk with brick dressings to hard slatestone and granite. Field names such as 'Quarry Field' or 'Brick Kiln Field' record their origin, and from the 1840s railways distributed many new ma-terials – most notably Welsh slate and machine brick.

Climate also affected building tech-niques. Celia Fiennes, on her visit to Devon and Cornwall in 1698, noted that in exposed coastal areas straw nets, weighed down with stones hanging from them, were laid over 'their ricks and outhouses': 'rope-thatch' was also used as protection against Atlantic gales in western Wales, Scotland and Ireland into the nineteenth century. Cement slurry on slate roofs provided further protection against fierce winds in these areas. South-west Wales, Scotland, and south-west England also have many barns and byres with scarfed-cruck roof trusses, made of two slight timbers joined to make a cruck shape, and timber-framed buildings are very rare. In Cornwall, a county of wind-bent trees and earth and stone hedges, the roof timbers of traditional farm build-ings are very slender (as little as 2 × 4 in for the main roof truss timbers) and so bay-lengths are reduced to as little as 1.5 m (5 ft). Leland, writing in the early sixteenth century, had commented on the shortage of timber and fuel in Corn-wall and he made virtually the same remark when he visited Swaledale in the Yorkshire Dales, where the field barns of Muker and Thwaite also have roofs of scrub oak: some purlins made of forked boughs occur, as in Cornwall or west Devon, because there was not enough timber to make continuous purlins (fig. 24.4).

Hedgerows grew elm for weather-

boarding and oaks for great timbers. Woodland management would certain-ly have affected the quality of timber from close-set standings which grew straight timbers, to parkland oak which provided timber for some of our largest cruck barns of which the fourteenth-century Leigh Court Barn near Worces-ter is the greatest. It is such great medieval barns that shall form the sub-ject of the next chapter.

26. *Cowhouse in Bransdale, Yorkshire* Early nineteenth-century cowhouse built of squared limestone with a pantile roof, typical of the East Yorkshire Moors. Such buildings replaced smaller cruck-roofed and heather-thatched farm buildings of which little trace now remains. There are steps to a first-floor fodder room in the gable end.

4
Cathedrals of Labour

GREAT medieval barns are still amongst the most impressive elements in the landscape. To the medieval peasant they represented the richness and power of their builders, the manorial lords and especially the wealthiest of over eight hundred religious communities who owned a quarter to one-fifth of the landed wealth of England at the time of their Dissolution by Henry VIII in 1538.

One of the finest medieval barns lies at Great Coxwell, which stands just to the south of Faringdon in Oxfordshire and was built for the Cistercian monks of Beaulieu Abbey between about 1275 and 1325. William Morris, high priest of the Arts and Crafts Movement, frequently took parties of friends to view the barn whilst he resided at Kelmscott Manor between 1871 and 1896. To Morris, a fervent medievalist, the barn was 'the finest piece of architecture in England, as beautiful as a cathedral'.

The resemblance was more than passing. The stone coping to the roof gables, the buttresses made of ashlared stone and, above all, its massive form with transeptal porch and pointed arched doorways, all serve as reminders that Great Coxwell's masons were versed in the newly imported traditions of Gothic architecture. Moreover, the interior is aisled, like a church.

Aisled construction, used from the Iron Age to build the farm houses of Northern Europe, was adopted by the emergent powers of post-Roman Europe to build palaces and churches, monastic barns and farm buildings. The remarkable eighth-century plan of the monastery of St Gall in Switzerland is crammed with aisled farm buildings; the aisled and timber-framed churches of Cheshire (such as Marton or Lower Peover) and early medieval aisled halls such as the Norman Bishop's Palace at Hereford shared the same tradition.

Aisled barns are concentrated nearest the Continent in southern and eastern England, very few occurring to the west of the limestone belt. If Cecil Hewett is correct in dating the original aisled barn at Belchamp St Paul's, Essex, to about AD 1020, aisled barns were used on Saxon estates. They had certainly become a familiar sight in twelfth-century Essex, where leases of St Paul's, London, make the church connection clear by referring to 'aisles' and 'naves' in the descriptions of their barns.

The use of aisles enables such barns to span great widths, in contrast to the long and narrow barns west of the

limestone belt. The aisled Great Coxwell barn is 13.36 m (43 ft 10 in) wide,
whereas the massive barn built in about
1400 at Abbotsbury in Dorset (fig. 33) is
81.9 m (272 ft) long but without the use
of aisles its width is restricted to 9.5 m
(31 ft). Frindsbury, at 64 m (210 ft), is
the longest medieval aisled barn in
Kent.

The roof at Great Coxwell is not only
supported by aisle posts but also by base
crucks, which spring from high in the

27.   *Great Coxwell Barn, Oxfordshire, c. 1300*
One of only three barns (the others are at
Shilton, Oxfordshire, and St Leonards,
Hampshire) that have survived out of 27
which the Cistercian monks of Beaulieu
Abbey owned in 1538. The porch has doveholes in its gable, accommodation for horses
in part of the ground floor and a room for a
granger, who supervised the barn's business, on the first floor. Photograph courtesy of The National Trust Photographic
Library/Nick Meers.

stone walls and meet a collar near the apex. Base crucks (see fig. 29) spanned a greater width than full crucks and prevented the floor from being cluttered with aisle posts. They are commonly found in medieval stone barns west of the limestone belt, as at Sherborne, Frocester Court, Gloucester, Glastonbury, Tewkesbury and Bath Abbeys. Some barns with base cruck roofs have aisled trusses at each end, as at Siddingham, the Bishop of Exeter's barn at Bishop's Clyst, Devon, and Middle Littleton, Worcestershire.

These great barns – larger than any built since – are still known as 'tithe barns'. Tithes, a levy by the church of one-tenth of the produce of its lay parishioners, originated as a payment in the seventh century to provide money for priests, church repair, and the poor. By the tenth century payment was made compulsory and tithes were divided between the lesser tithe on young farmstock, poultry, bees, vegetables and the like and the great tithe which was taken from the corn crop: this was stored in the tithe barn adjoining the parish church. In 1836 an Act for England and Wales commuted tithes into a rent charge, but they remained a burden and great source of annoyance to farmers until – after protests and petitions – they were finally abolished in 1936.

Many barns stand on land granted by Saxon kings and lords, but in the twelfth century a religious revival led to a great increase in endowments of land

28. *Interior of Great Coxwell Barn, Oxfordshire, c. 1300*
Note the division into central nave and side aisles. The roof trusses are supported by aisle posts from which three-way braces strengthen the tie beams and wall plates; between each pair of aisle posts, base crucks spring from high in the wall to provide additional support to the roof. Photograph courtesy of the Royal Commission on the Historical Monuments of England.

to religious foundations. Invariably, such gifts included the advowson of the parish church – this being the right to nominate the incumbent priest and to collect tithes – which was augmented in later years by the gift or purchase of neighbouring pieces of land. Tithes therefore became an important source of revenue: thus the tithe barn at Siddingham, Gloucestershire, was built soon after the site was acquired by Knights Hospitallers in the early thirteenth century, and the Grange Barn at Coggeshall, Essex, was built immediately after the Cistercian Coggeshall Abbey was founded by King Stephen in 1140. The barn at Great Coxwell stands on one of the manors granted in 1203 by King John to the Cistercians as an endowment for a new monastic community at Faringdon, but the site was deemed unsuitable by the Cistercians who moved to Beaulieu in Hampshire. The further acquisition by Beaulieu Abbey of the churches of Shilton (where part of a Beaulieu barn remains) and Inglesham in 1243, bringing more tithes, made barns for the reception of produce more essential.

High Farming and the Cistercians

The Cistercians, founded in 1098, were by far the most important and influential of the new monastic orders that had emerged out of the fragmentation of the ancient Benedictine order. In contrast to the Benedictines, who lived by receiving manorial rents and dues, the Cistercians, determined to be free of worldly cares and set aside more time for their spiritual life, established their own farms known as granges – after *'grangius'* the Latin word for barn. Some of these farms were dispersed about open fields and worked by bond labour, but most broke with such traditional practice because they were compact 'ring-fence' farms run along modern lines. These were initially staffed by lay brethren, peasants working under a simple monastic rule who were answerable to the cellarer based at the head abbey.

The barn at Great Coxwell, therefore, stored the produce of an enclosed working farm which extended for hundreds of acres. Its regular staff in the fourteenth century included a swineherd, eight ploughmen and two carters, beside a cheese maker, a baker, a hayward and a forester. At harvest time, the tithe-collector was only one amongst the extra staff, which included a cowherd, three shepherds, a cook and his boy.

These labourers may have slept with their animals in byres or stables, but more commonly the typical grange had a communal hall, a kitchen and a sleeping chamber. The demands of seasonal farm labour and increased disturbance and even riots amongst their lay brethren meant that few granges could be completely isolated or manage without wage or bond labour. In Yorkshire, the Fountains Grange of Kirby Wiske was sited next to the parish church, and the earthworks of peasant dwellings can be found to the east of the more isolated Jervaulx grange at Braithwaite.

Fountains Abbey owned twenty granges: these included the cattle lodges (vaccaries) of Nidderdale, which formed part of a closely integrated system, Fountains moving the cattle between estates and exporting hides to Newcastle. The Cistercians managed other vaccaries in the Fenlands, the southwest and around the fortified garrison towns of north Wales. At Dean Moor, Dartmoor, archaeologists have discovered a former grange of Buckfast Abbey built between about 1200 and 1350 as a cattle lodge for tending stock in summer. Stock enclosures stood next to a nearby river, and the grange had a house and large byre which flanked a central enclosed yard; the lay brother

slept in the house and the herdsman in the byre. The Cistercians were also leading wool producers, exporting to Italy and the Netherlands. Meaux Abbey, for example, owned 14,000 sheep on its Yorkshire estates.

These Cistercian granges spearheaded the colonisation of marginal land, and the massive proportions of their surviving barns bear witness to the great expansion of population and cereal production between 1100 and 1300 (p. 16). Walter Map wrote in the thirteenth century that they 'level everything before the ploughshare', and pollen analysis has revealed that the monks of Strata Florida in south Wales (founded 1146) ploughed up land that had been rough grazing since at least the Iron Age. At Monknash Grange in Glamorgan stand the ruins of the largest known barn in Wales, and Beaulieu Abbey's aisled barn at St Leonard's in Hampshire, had a larger storage capacity (14,913 cu m or 526,590 cu ft) than any known barn: it was 68.2 m (224 ft) long and 20.4 m (67 ft) wide, and its ruins can still be seen towering over the road that passes through the village. Smaller Cistercian barns were built in about 1280 at Boxley, Kent, and about 1300 at Calcot, Gloucestershire.

By about 1230, the Cistercian example had already inspired other holy orders and laymen to bring their lands under direct management and consolidate their estates into 'ring-fence' farms, spurred on by population pressure and inflation which, between 1180 and 1220, had seen corn and livestock prices treble and the real value of rented estates plummet. Many Benedictine abbeys now invested in large improvement schemes, such as Glastonbury Abbey's draining of the Somerset Levels or Geoffrey of Crowland's improvement of waste lands owned by Peterborough Abbey (1299–1320). One of the most remarkable improvers of his day was Prior Henry of Eastrey of

Canterbury Cathedral Priory, who in 37 years of office at the end of the thirteenth century spent £3,739 on building and repairs besides extra sums of money on draining, marling, liming and even medicine for livestock.

Their cattle lodges (vaccaries) and barns now rivalled those of the Cistercians. For example, the vaccary at Barnard Castle, Durham, had 300 cattle and calves in 1326. The thirteenth-century Great Barn at Cholsey, Berkshire, on a former royal estate given to Reading Abbey, was, at 92.4 m (303 ft) long, one of the longest buildings in Europe until its demolition in 1815. Of the aisled barns of the south-east, we can include within the period of expansion between 1200 and 1350 Court Lodge, Brook, for Christ Church, Canterbury, and Littlebourne and Lenham barns (the latter having been carbon dated to 1330–45) built for St Augustine's, Canterbury.

The fertile soils of the south east, and particularly coastal Sussex, were ideal for arable farming, and by 1300 most of the estate lands of the Archbishop of Canterbury and Battle Abbey were set in 'ring-fence' farms, which practised advanced forms of crop rotation and increasing use of legumes on fallow land, which restored fertility by fixing nitrogen back into the soil; the folding of sheep and cattle, fed on the lush pastures at the heads of inlets and estuaries, manured the land well. A sheep house erected by Battle Abbey measured 30.5 × 4.26 m (100 × 14 ft) and, like all medieval sheep houses, has not survived, but at Alciston, Battle Abbey's home farm which managed over 1,000 acres of land, there stands a fourteenth-century barn; this fine barn is aisled, the aisled trusses alternating with trusses having large curved braces which spring from post to collar, and is situated near a medieval dovecote and church south of the village. Another barn, at Adderbury in Oxfordshire,

was probably first built by the Bishop of Winchester in the early 1300s: the estate was directly managed, and its four open fields grew wheat, rye, oats and spring barley and, like an increasing number of areas in the thirteenth century, the fallow land was sown with peas which restored fertility.

The great thirteen-bay base cruck barn at Frocester, Gloucestershire, was built between 1294 and 1306 for Abbot John de Gamages of Gloucester Abbey. The finest group of base-cruck barns was built in the fourteenth century for Glastonbury Abbey (Benedictine), which owned property in Hampshire, Berkshire and Devon as well as more locally in Wiltshire, Dorset and Somerset. The exterior of the Abbey Barn on the Abbey's home farm in Glastonbury has carved trefoils and quatrefoils, an ogee-headed window over the porch, carved symbols of the Evangelists and carved heads, said to be benefactors of the Abbey. The roofless barn at Pilton also has carved symbols of the Evangelists, and quatrefoils act as owlholes at the smaller five-bay barn at West Pennard which has doveholes in its gable end. The most imposing of this group is surely at Doulting, an eight-bay barn with two sets of transeptal porches and graceful cruciform ventilation slits piercing massively buttressed walls. It was not only built to store tithes (the church had been appropriated in the 1260s) but also formed the centre of a manorial estate which by the fourteenth century comprised 357 acres of arable, 80 acres of meadow and 118 acres of pasture.

The exterior of the Doulting Barn invites comparison with another great early fourteenth-century barn, the Shaftesbury Abbey barn at Bradford-on-Avon which has a magnificent roof of raised crucks similar to the smaller barn at Lacock Abbey, also built for Benedictine nuns. The largest cruck barn in the world at Leigh Court near

Worcester, built for Pershore Abbey, is also early fourteenth century and has massive full crucks spanning 10.2 m (33 ft 5 in) internally.

Further north, the great aisled fourteenth-century barn at Bolton Priory (now known as Bolton Abbey) in Yorkshire served an estate which grew more corn than grass until the late fifteenth century – in stark contrast to the Craven Dales today. At Bolton itself, which is 400 ft above sea level, the Priory had 800 acres of arable – mostly oats – which it directly cultivated between 1295 and 1325. Over 100 full-time '*famuli*' (farmworkers) lived in cow byres or their own cottages with attached allotments. The home farm's oxhouse accommodated 80 to 100 oxen which pulled the 8 ploughs used to cultivate this estate and up to 500 cattle were accommodated in nearby vaccaries, their hides being sold for export. Most of the corn stored in the barn was used to feed the animals, the household and the farm staff, and make ale from malted oats. Sales of wool accounted for one-half of the Priory's cash income, and the foundations of its sheephouses can still be traced on Malham Moor.

There is less evidence of improvements by secular lords. The Earl of Hereford built a seven-bay base cruck barn at Southam, Gloucestershire, in the early 1300s. Henry de Bray, a lesser Northamptonshire landlord, recorded his building work and acquisition of surrounding property in his own hand.

29. Interior of the Abbey Barn, Glastonbury, Somerset (and inset of porch)
Recent dendrochronological dating has dated the barn to between 1341 and 1363. The two-tier base-cruck roof is of seven bays and of similar construction to Doulting and West Pennard barns. The barns at Preston Plucknett and Pilton complete the group. Photograph courtesy of Stephen James.

To the existing farm buildings, which included a cattle house, he added a pigsty and fowl house in 1298, a new barn in 1301, a sheephouse in 1302, a dovecote in 1303, a granary and sheepfold in 1304 and a cartshed in 1307.

These great barns reflected increasing interest in the profitable management of estates, and medieval accounts bear witness to the regular maintenance work needed to keep them in good repair. Each manor or farm was run by the reeve or bailiff, who submitted his accounts each year. Many bishops, abbots and lords had built up sophisticated and centralised accounting systems by 1300, often staffed by professional stewards who had served for other abbeys and who replaced former sub-tenants as administrators. The steward of St Swithin's Priory, Winchester, visited each manor twice a year and senior monks were appointed as auditors to advise on the purchase of stock and land management: the accounts here included the tough '*responsio*' whereby the reeve was expected to meet a fixed return from his land or stock – if he did not, he had to pay the difference.

Guides for managers, like Walter of Henley's *Book of Husbandry*, appeared in the thirteenth century. He advised estates to appoint officials (either reeves or grangers) to record sales of grain from barns. Grangers were accommodated over the porches of many medieval barns, as at Great Coxwell. The porch at Bredon Barn, Worcestershire, has an external staircase and an octagonal chimneystack serving a fireplace inside the reeve's or granger's first-floor chamber and at Abbotsbury Barn, Dorset, a well-appointed chamber is reached by an external stairturret.

Medieval barns were efficiently managed. Lease agreements dated 1114 of the Essex estates of St Paul's, London, record arrangements for storage in meticulous detail: their barn at Wicham, for example, was to be 'full of summer wheat from the entrance toward the east, and from the entrance toward the west it must be full of oats'. The 300 acre manorial farm at Cuxham, Oxfordshire, had a barn for spring corn and a barn for wheat, and the remarkable Barley Barn of about 1200–20 and Wheat Barn of about 1275–85 at Cressing Temple, Essex, reflect a similar arrangement. Medieval barns were often used to store beans and peas as well as cereals.

The marketing of produce from barns also assumed greater importance from the thirteenth century. The monastic grange at Waltham Abbey, Essex, was in an excellent position to export as it adjoined the river Lea: a wharf and dock stood north of the barn, which in the thirteenth century had been extended to twelve bays. Sales of agricultural produce amounted to about two-thirds of the manorial revenue from the Archbishop of Canterbury's estates, and about 50 per cent of the Abbey and Bishopric of Ely's estates in 1251. Ely's main market was King's Lynn and the coastal trade, and Canterbury even exported to France if the

30. *Middle Littleton Tithe Barn, Worcestershire*

The only survivor of 'Eight magnificent granges' built between 1296 and 1316 by Abbot John De Brokehampton of Evesham Abbey who rebuilt many churches and even built canals during his term of office. Photograph courtesy of The National Trust/Martin Charles.

31. *Bredon Barn, Worcestershire (left)*

Built for the Bishop of Worcester in the fourteenth century. Note the chimney which served the granger's chamber. The barn lay to the west of a courtyard which was surrounded by stables for horses and plough oxen, a granary, pigsty, sheepcote, poultry house and dovecote.

price was good; in August 1348, 1,000 quarters of wheat were threshed out in the Archbishop of Canterbury's barns and exported to Calais.

These great barns have survived, mainly owing to their size and high quality, but were not the only buildings which served medieval estates. In the fourteenth and fifteenth centuries the farm buildings on the Bishop of Winchester's grange at Adderbury, Oxfordshire, included a malthouse, brewhouse, granary, hay barn, pighouse, oxhouse and sheepcote. Fishponds, rabbit warrens and dovecotes also produced plentiful supplies of fresh food. The prior of Dunstable built seven dovecotes on his land between

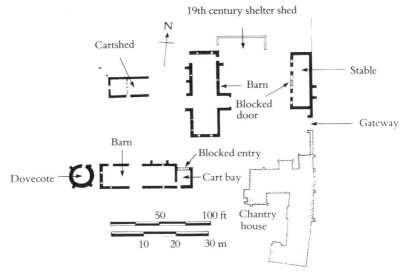

19th century shelter shed

N

Cartshed

Stable

Barn

Blocked
door

Gateway

Barn

Blocked entry

Dovecote

Cart bay

50   100 ft

10   20   30 m

Chantry
house

32. *Stoke-sub-Hamdon, Somerset*
Photo The Chantry House and farm buildings are built of local Ham Hill stone with thatch roofs. Many of the buildings are now roofless, or have late eighteenth-century roof trusses.
Plan (left) The chantry house was rebuilt in the fifteenth century and includes its own chapel and dormitory. It lies to the south of a farmyard entered by a buttressed gateway to the east. Plan redrawn by courtesy of Astam Design Partnership, Gloucester.

1248 and 1273, and the dovecote at Kinwarton, Warwickshire, is one surviving example of many dovecotes built by Evesham Abbey (fig. 17). Abbot Roger Yatton rebuilt many cowsheds on the Evesham estates between 1379 and 1418.

Granaries, accommodation for plough beasts and other buildings were usually built around one or two courtyards. The early fourteenth-century barn at Bradford-on-Avon, Wiltshire, stands to the south of a yard surrounded by a house to the north, a cruck-built granary (probably fourteenth century) to the east and the ruins of another medieval farm building, probably a byre, to the west.

One of the most complete groups of medieval farm buildings lies at Stoke-sub-Hamdon, Somerset. In 1304 the Beauchamp family, lords of the manor, founded a collegiate chantry of four brethren or chaplains headed by a provost whose function was to pray for their lordships' souls. To ensure that these memorial masses could be performed in perpetuity, the Beauchamps gave the chantry lands and the advowson of the church, two-thirds of the tithes going to support the chaplains and a further one-third for the vicar. The farm buildings were erected to store the tithes and serve the chantry lands in the village's open fields, which grew everything from wheat, oats and barley to beans and peas. The group is divided into two courtyards by a barn. The stable, altered in the nineteenth century, is at least seventeenth century in origin and probably stands on the site of a former medieval stable or oxhouse. The outer court buildings include a barn with a cartshed (later altered to house livestock) added to its east end, a dovecote with about 500 nesting holes and a cartshed or open-fronted sheephouse originally floored over (probably by a granary).

The Decline of the Great Barn

By the early 1300s, however, the encroachment of arable had led to a shortage of grassland for feeding livestock which provided essential manure to fertilise the land. Exhaustion of corn lands led to lower yields in some areas, which contributed towards the famines of the early 1300s (see pp. 16–17) and imposed limits on the amounts of cash that could be invested in estates: indeed, investment schemes such as those undertaken by Henry of Eastrey were limited to no more than 5 per cent of net expenditure. Moreover, many estates were too small or scattered to facilitate direct management.

By the time that the Black Death arrived in 1349, wiping out a third of the population at once, many smaller abbeys – badly affected by the agrarian crisis of 30 years previously – had already abandoned their policies of direct management and found more financial security in leasing out their estates. A short-term recovery was followed by further plagues and epidemics which led to a labour shortage and wage rises, prompting more leasing and the gradual changeover from the emphasis on arable farming to less labour-intensive sheep or cattle farming in the fifteenth century.

Leasing out barns with their tithes for money rents also reduced transport and other costs. Thus, fifteen barns had been under the direct control of Leicester Abbey in the fourteenth century, but their numbers were reduced by leasing to eight in 1477 and four in 1538; Bredon Barn was leased out after 1410, half of Middle Littleton Barn was leased out by 1538 and the monks of Beaulieu let Great Coxwell barn to their bailiff, Thomas Mores, in 1531. The fields around Alciston barn on Battle Abbey's home farm had grown the farm's biggest acreage of corn in the 1380s and

1390s, but the income from sales of produce had fallen by nearly one-third by the 1470s; in 1496 the barn was leased out. The Benedictine nuns of Lacock Abbey had held on to most of their demesne until as late as 1476, but like most other landlords, they had leased out all but their home farm (where the cruck barn in Lacock now stands) by 1535.

Home farms remained to provide food for their owners, and this explains

the building of fifteenth-century barns on home farms at Michelham Priory in East Sussex, Buckland in Devon, Abbotsbury in Dorset and Tisbury in Wiltshire. The Tisbury estate, home farm of the Benedictine nuns of Shaftesbury Abbey, had grown to 1400 acres by 1380 when the nuns were given licence to 'appropriate' (acquire) the church: in the early fifteenth century they built a new grange which included a fine new barn, 57.3 m (188 ft) long,

33. *Abbotsbury Barn, Dorset*
Built in about 1400 on the home farm of Abbotsbury Abbey. The barn is one of the longest in England, but is now roofed for only half of its original length of 81.9 m (272 ft).

two gatehouses and a stable block (de-molished) which divided the complex into two yards. Little could be done, however, to arrest the decay of farm buildings on other estates that had been leased out since the late thirteenth cen-tury.

The change to pasture farming bene-fited wealthier yeomen and lay lords, and many villages were destroyed in the fifteenth century to make way for sheep grazings. Significantly, a sheep's head is moulded on one of the terracotta pla-ques that grace the moated set of brick outbuildings at Crows Hall, Debenham in Suffolk: these were built for Bassing-bourn Gawdy, a wealthy grazier who had 10 flocks of sheep each numbering 450 to 700.

Brick was a fashionable new material from Flanders and Flemish craftsmen were often imported to build in brick. Sir James Hobart, a successful lawyer who served as Attorney General and member of the Privy Council to Henry VII, bought and remodelled Hales Hall, Norfolk, as his country seat and built his barn and house in brick. The crow-stepped gables used at Hales Barn were another Flemish feature which became popular in East Anglia by the seven-teenth century, as at Dersingham in Norfolk where a fine stone barn with brick details is dated 1671. Two note-able examples with crow-stepped gables stand at Willington in Bedford-shire, where Sir John Gostwick, Car-dinal Wolsey's Master of the Horse, built a fine stable and dovecote (with about 1500 nesting holes) in about 1540.

He had bought the manor in 1529, and erected these buildings using materials from nearby Newnham Priory which had been dissolved in 1536.

Men such as Gostwick had benefited from the Dissolution of the Monasteries between 1536 and 1538 and the consequent dispersal of their estates. The late sixteenth-century barn at Winterborne Clenston in Dorset has a fine roof of seven fifteenth-century hammer-beam trusses taken from Milton Abbey after its Dissolution in 1538. With the passing of the monasteries and chantries the medieval age had come to an end, and the reins of power were now firmly in the hands of farmers, secular lords, merchants and lawyers.

Between 1562 and 1577 Sir Thomas Gresham, the famous financier of Eliza-

beth I's reign, built a new brick mansion at Osterley Park in Middlesex, providing a brick barn and stables built around three sides of a courtyard facing his house. Gresham, no doubt, would have been well acquainted with Flanders brick, as he divided his time between London and the financial centre of Antwerp before he sold his house there in 1574. His Antwerp agent had been Sir Richard Clough, a merchant and son of a Welsh glover, who at the same time built a Flemish-style house and range of outbuildings, mainly in brick, at Bachegraig, Tremeirchion in Clwyd. These were to be the storage centre of Clough's trading operations in North Wales (which never bore fruit) and the courtyard of buildings includes a cart-shed, cowhouse, stable or oxhouse and part of a barn. Clough had imported workmen and materials from Antwerp in 1561 to build his merchants' exchange in London, and it is likely that Bachegraig followed suit in 1567, for its bricks are not local to the area.

There can be no doubt that Bachegraig, although exceptional, showed that commercially orientated lay farmers – and not the medieval ecclesiastical estates – were now in the forefront of change. The great eleven-bay barn at Gunthwaite, Yorkshire, was built in about 1550 for Sir Godfrey Bosville, and when Sir William Paston had his name inscribed on his barn at Paston in Norfolk, erected in 1581, he thereby asserted the new-found strength of his own class.

34. *Hales Barn, Hales Hall, Norfolk*
Built for Sir James Hobart in about 1480, the barn is over 54.8 m (180 ft) long and is made of over 700,000 bricks. The chimney in the east end served the chamber of Hobart's Master of the Horse, which adjoins a twelve-horse stable and has a crown-post roof in the chamber above. The barn occupies the south side of a large courtyard, which has an embattled wall to the east and Hobart's house and gatehouse to the north.

5
Yeoman and Peasant

HE word 'peasant' is a term rather loosely coined for any countryman. Its most strict definition is of a family of cultivators who grow enough food to feed themselves – for which about 10–15 acres (4–6 hectares) would suffice, depending on soil, climate and the availability of common land. No labour outside the family would be employed, although some produce would be sent to market. This chapter will examine the difference between the farm buildings of peasants and wealthier yeomen farmers, and the eventual division between the small highland farmstead and the larger lowland farmstead of mixed or cereal farming regions.

The Longhouse Tradition

The simplest type of peasant farmstead was the longhouse, where people and animals shared the same entrance and lived at opposite ends of the same building. The longhouse has an ancestry which reaches back over six thousand years into the Neolithic, the age when settled farming began. The most simple type of longhouse, the byre-dwelling, was used by peasantry in poorer parts of Europe into the 1900s. Bishop Hall, in the sixteenth century, regarded the one-room house as typical of the northern farmer:

*Of one bay's breadth, God wot! a silly cote
. . .
At his bed's feet feeden his stalled team
His swine beneath, his pullen o'er the beam*

Chaucer, in the fourteenth century, described a similar cottage in the *Nuns' Priest's Tale* where fowl roosted on the beams. In Germany the tie beam was known as the '*Hahnebalken*' or fowl beam, and in Ireland the superstition that it was unlucky for a card player to sit beneath a tie beam was, like most traditions, rooted in common sense.

In Northumberland, simple byre-dwellings were used into the eighteenth century. Excavations at West Whelpington (deserted in about 1720) have shown that between the fifteenth and seventeenth centuries the village consisted of longhouses grouped about a green, with some haystacks on stone bases and small outbuildings for storage. The longhouses were of one storey and built of stone rubble with cruck-framed and heather-thatch roofs. At the dwelling end, the fire burned on a central hearth, smoking out humans and cattle alike, for no partition except a hanging cloth or cupboard seems to have divided the humans from the cattle, which faced the side walls. Only after 1665, when a new landlord replanned the village, was there some improvement with the reduction of five farmsteads to three, and each longhouse was rebuilt with extra cattle accommodated in a longer byre – 10 m (32 ft 10 in) as opposed to 5 m – separated by a stone partition from the dwelling. In Ireland the byre end was rarely partitioned off before the nineteenth century and then only with a cupboard – surely a reflection of the ancient Irish belief that cattle would increase their milk yield if kept in sight of the hearth fire.

Continued use of these simple byre-dwellings in Northumberland and Ireland can be (partly at least) explained by the small size and poverty of peasant holdings caused by strong landlord control and the survival of partible inheritance, by which all sons received equal shares of land as co-heirs. Six-

teenth-century Northumbrian farms were remarkable for the uniformity of their size (20–30 acres or 8.1–11.2 hectares). This firmly shut the lid on peasant enterprise, unlike other areas which practised the same custom such as East Anglia and Kent where the predominance of freeholders, better marketing facilities and woodland industries (such as in the Weald of Kent and Sussex) had led to more opportunities for individual enterprise and great variety of house types and farm sizes by the sixteenth century. Nineteenth-century Ulster settlements which prac-

35. *Fourteenth-century longhouse, Wharram Percy, Yorkshire* The true longhouse had the same entrance for people and cattle via a through-passage at the byre end, their quarters being separated by a low partition wall, usually of timber frame. The cattle would either face and be fed from the through-passage or stand facing the side walls of the byre (as shown here). From *Man made the Land*, David and Charles, 1973. *Geographical Magazine.*

tised partible inheritance and a simple 'infield–outfield' system of highland farming were, like West Whelpington, characterised by clusters of byre dwellings of the same size. Significantly, it was left to powerful landlords from the eighteenth century to clear such settlements and plant new farmsteads out in the fields (see pp. 119–20).

In more socially fluid areas, however, longhouses embraced a wider social range and from the medieval period were built by wealthier farmers who could accommodate twelve or so milking cattle in their byres in contrast to the four or five owned by the peasants of West Whelpington or Ulster. The farmers of Hound Tor on Dartmoor, for example, tended their stock and grew cereals at 1,200 feet above sea level until deteriorating climate and the Black Death forced them to abandon the site in the fourteenth century; the house platforms and field systems of the village can still be seen today. The buildings of this former 'shieling' (see p. 15) were rebuilt in stone in about 1200 and included longhouses, small barns and corn-drying kilns, as well as a longhouse and two barns built inside a Bronze Age pound. The longhouses already showed a widening social gulf, from the smallest at 8.2 × 3 m (27 × 10 ft) to the largest at 15.5 × 4.6 m (51 × 15 ft) which had a stone wall dividing men from beasts. Similarly, at Wharram Percy in Yorkshire the longhouses ranged between 15.2 m (50 ft) and 27.4 m (90 ft) long.

Another thirteenth-century Dartmoor longhouse, complete with stone outbuilding and corn-drying kiln, was excavated at Beere: it was made of stone and was built – like the larger longhouses of Hound Tor and Wharram Percy – to a three-room plan, with a hall flanked by a through-passage and byre at the lower end and a sleeping room at the upper end. This three-room plan, complete with through-passage as wide

as 8 ft to facilitate the manoeuvres of horned cattle, formed the basis of the classic longhouse. Early examples would have been of open-hall type, with the fire burning on a hearth on the hall floor and low wood partitions separating the hall from inner and outer rooms. This would have been the plan at Black Daren, Llanveynoe, a fifteenth-century stone cruck-built longhouse in the Black Mountains of the Herefordshire borders: there was no division between hall and through-passage, and the mortice holes for tethering posts on the underside of the tie beam between byre and passage suggest that the farmer fed his cattle from the passage. This is a typical feature of early longhouses. At Chapple, Gidleigh, on the east side of Dartmoor, stands a small hamlet of two early sixteenth-century longhouses and a

row of barns of similar date. One of these longhouses is well preserved and shows that cattle were fed from the passage; the cowhouse also had a loading door to a hay loft which had removable joists enabling hay to be dropped to the cattle below. Other Dartmoor longhouses, such as fifteenth-century Uppacott, near Poundsgate, had cattle facing the side walls – a less convenient arrangement.

These improved longhouses show that longhouses were accepted at a high social level, and were not the symbols of poverty that byre-dwellings had become. Ancient pastoral societies – especially the Celts – held their cattle in high esteem and longhouses continued to be built by men of local note. Rees Williams (d. 1621), for example, built a longhouse at Trebanog Fach, Breconshire, in about 1600 and so shared the

36. *Shilstone Farmhouse, Throwleigh, Devon* One of the finest Dartmoor longhouses. It was built into a slope (with the cattle at the lower end) and to the traditional three-unit plan in about 1500: at that date the hall, heated by an open hearth, was divided from the shippon (cowhouse) to right and inner room to left by low partitions. The chimneystacks, including one backing onto the through passage, and first floors were inserted after about 1600. The fine front door is inscribed RT 1656, when a separate entry was made to the shippon: the cattle faced the side walls, and backed onto a central dung channel which had an outlet in the gable wall. The cowhouse is attached to an eighteenth-century stable. A dung pit with old stone walls stands in the centre of the yard, flanked by the longhouse to one side and a seventeenth-century barn, cowhouse and linhay on the other side.

same entrance as his cattle. It is even possible, according to Peter Smith, that the owner of Tŷ-Mawr, Castell Caerenion, Monmouthshire, a fine fifteenth-century hall-house with cusped woodwork to its aisled and base cruck roof, could sit at his high table and proudly view his cattle feeding beyond the passage.

After about 1600, many of these longhouses were refurbished to the latest standards of domestic comfort. In the fifteenth century, for example, the typical Breconshire longhouse was a low timber-framed building set into a slope, often with a mucking-out door in the lower gable end; from the late sixteenth century, the hall might be rebuilt in stone, a chimney built against the through-passage, a loft inserted and a separate door made to the byre. Typically, longhouses thus altered have a tall house to one side of a low byre and the two sections often belong to different periods of rebuilding. Surviving examples of these improved longhouses are concentrated in south Wales, Dartmoor, the Lake District and the hillsides of the Shropshire and Herefordshire borders. Spout House, a fine seventeenth-century 'true longhouse' with a single entry, can be seen in the Ryedale Folk Museum in the North Yorkshire Moors. By the seventeenth century some farmsteads with longhouses had extensive ranges of outbuildings, especially barns and cowhouses for extra cattle (fig. 36).

It was this two-storey plan, with chimney backing onto passage, which became adopted by Cumbrian farmers to build their longhouses from the 1660s to the end of the eighteenth century. Early examples have no partition between byre and passage, but in later examples the passage is flanked by full-height stone walls and the shippon might also be given a separate entrance, as at Nettleslack, Martindale, dated 1735.

The lower room would have been used for cattle only in winter and inventories show that it could also have served as a store for fishing gear or farm implements. The typical Northumbrian one-storey longhouse as described in the eighteenth century had its 'in-bye' which served as inner sanctum for the family and its 'out-bye' which served as byre in winter and bedroom and store in summer.

The next logical step was to separate byre from house. In Cheshire, the Vale of York and much of the Dales, North Wales and Cornwall it is certain that no true longhouses were built after 1600. The tradition, however, is reflected in the multitude of linear farmsteads, where farm buildings are attached to but separate from farmhouses, in the north and west of Britain, and the popularity of the three-unit plan with through passage in south Wales, the West Midlands, Devon and the limestone belt from North Riding to Dorset coast. The linear farmstead is also found on the fringes of the limestone zone, such as the Cotswolds, and even as far east as the Chilterns.

Another form of combined dwelling/farm building had appeared in Lancashire and west Yorkshire by the 1650s. These, known as laithe-houses after the local term for barn which was 'lathe' or 'laithe', were built with separate entries for men and beasts and were especially popular in the south Pennines where no seventeenth-century longhouses have been recorded. The Bankhouse at Luddenden, Halifax, is inscribed 'Built by Gilbert Brokesbank 1650' over the door and has fine arched doorways and moulded windows. Lane Head Laithe, Carleton, may be early seventeenth century; the laithe had a cruck roof which has been since removed, and probably originated as a cowhouse for housing cattle which grazed on the common fields.

Many nineteenth-century laithe houses,

such as those around Pateley Bridge, had small dwelling areas – often no more than two-up, two-down – and provision for six cattle and a hay mow in the laithe. They were used by small-holders who worked in lead mining or the cloth industry, of the type described by James Caird in 1851: 'When trade is good the farm is neglected, when trade is dull the weaver becomes a more attentive farmer'. Part-time farmers were building such laithe-houses until as late as 1880 and their farmyards, which served holdings no greater than 50 acres, might be equipped with a pump, kennel, pigsties and two-horse stable with cartshed: in the 1720s, Daniel Defoe had commented that such

37. *Laithe house south of Penistone, south Yorkshire* The typical laithe house was built of high-quality masonry, often of ashlar at the front. The cow stalls were separated from the dwelling by a stone partition wall and storage for hay (called the hay mow). This early nineteenth century laithe house was extended by the addition of another cowhouse in about 1860.

farmers 'scarce sow enough corn for their cocks and hens'. Relatively few laithe houses have been recorded in east Yorkshire, where farms were larger and grew more corn.

Lowland England and the Courtyard Plan

The higher unit cost of arable farming in lowland areas encouraged the growth of larger farms which employed wage labour and were geared to the London market (see pp. 88–91). As early as 1577 Thomas Harrison, in his description of England, noted the distinction between the smaller family hill farms of the north and west which had farmhouses attached to farm buildings, and the farmsteads built around courtyards found on larger farms, especially in the wealthier south and east.

In the open-field parishes of England, the traditional peasant holding or 'yard-land' of 15 to 30 acres (6–12 hectares) had been fragmented by inheritance customs and population pressure by the late thirteenth century. Many peasants sold their land to wealthier customary tenants who might own as much as 50 to 80 acres(20–32 hectares) and sub-let their lands. For example, the Gere and Le Wro families busily acquired land and by the 1340s were two of only eight interrelated families who owned all the land in the parish of Boroughby on the Peterborough Abbey estates.

A major consequence of the drop in population after the Black Death was acquisition by wealthier peasant farmers of deserted holdings, a speedier replacement of the old customary labour service by cash rents and an increase of sub-letting and inter-peasant loans. Half the lessees of the Archbishop of Canterbury's demesnes were yeomen, who by about 1400 cultivated about 60–80 acres (24–32 hectares) of land as against 30 acres at most in 1341. In open-field areas, yeomen farmers

might exchange and consolidate their scattered strips of land and make their own enclosed farms. The self-interest of a few market-orientated wealthy peasants now conflicted with communal farming – a development noted by many historians. At Durrington, a chalkland village in Wiltshire, the thirteenth century saw the emergence of a 'new group of large-scale tenants' of the Winchester College estate, such as the Martyns, who were engaged in large-scale farming selling livestock, corn and wool to Salisbury market: this brought them into conflict with their poor neighbours and they were constantly 'arraigned' for overstocking common land with their animals.

Such changes have been well summarised by Christopher Dyer in his study of Warwickshire farming between 1350 and 1520.

Before 1349 large holdings of more than thirty acres were rare; by 1520 they had become commonplace. Very large units of hundreds of acres were managed by lords before the mid-fourteenth century, but most of them were in the hands of tenant-farmers in the early sixteenth century. Before 1349 both peasants and lords concentrated on arable cultivation: by 1520 a balance between arable and pasture had emerged and graziers exploited specialist farms. New techniques such as the use of leys, flexible landuse, variable rotations, and enclosure were all disseminated in our period.

The Dissolution of the Monasteries, moreover, enabled such farmers to purchase their land.

These yeomen farmers marked their wealth by building detached farmhouses and buildings around yards, as extra accommodation for corn and stock became necessary. At Wharram Percy in Yorkshire, for example, only the manorial farmstead was built around a yard: the other farmers in the village lived in longhouses. However, there is no evidence that longhouses were used in East Anglia at all. A thirteenth-century longhouse excavated at Hangleton in Sussex, with a byre comparable in size – 2 × 2.75 m (6 ft 7 in by 9 ft) to nineteenth-century Ulster examples, had been demolished to make way for a courtyard farm in the fourteenth century. At Gomeldon, in Wiltshire, a longhouse was rebuilt and extended until by 1300 it had become a farmstead with detached house and its own barn, byre and yard.

The emergence of courtyard farms by the fourteenth century has also been

38. *Linear farmstead, Harwood Head, Northumberland* A late eighteenth-century farmhouse with a six-cow byre, three-horse stable and loosebox attached to the right. Further to right, an early nineteenth-century twelve-cow byre with doveholes in the gable end and a Victorian addition. To the rear, a privy, ash pit, coal house and pigsties.

noted at Thuxton (Norfolk), Upton (Gloucestershire), Faxton and Wythemail (Northamptonshire). In the fifteenth century, longhouses were replaced by courtyard farms at Barton Blount, in Derbyshire, paralleled by the emergence in the area of rich local merchants breeding cattle for sale as fatstock. Many farmers in the Weald of Kent, for example, had detached cowhouses and aisled three to five bay barns serving mixed corn and cattle farms of between 60 and 120 acres. Thus Bridge Farm, at Bridge in Kent, had an entry at one side of the house to a yard flanked by a fifteenth-century cowhouse and barn. Farm buildings built around yards became the hallmark of wealthier farms in many areas. On highland hill farms, until enclosures and improvements from the late eighteenth century, farms built around yards or with detached ranges of farm buildings were invariably those of gentry status (see fig. 1.4).

By contrast, we have seen that farmers north and west of the limestone belt (especially in northern England and Wales) continued to build linear farm-

39.   *Linear farmstead in Caernarvonshire* This is probably late seventeenth-century, and includes a cruck-roofed cowhouse. The house, originally of one storey, was converted into a two-storey house in about 1910.

steads with farmhouse and attached buildings. A gentleman of East Anglia or the south-east would have been aghast that Braithwaite Hall in Yorkshire, dated 1667, lies next to a range of pigsties and has a byre attached to the rear. In the East Riding, a farmhouse dated 1745 in Bransdale has a byre attached to the lower end and a Victorian extension connecting the other gable to an eighteenth-century barn, thus underlining the persistence of the longhouse tradition.

Therefore, the contrast still remains between the larger and mostly lowland farmstead, whose farmhouse might have its own driveway and face away from the yard, and the workaday character of the northern and western hill farm where a visitor might only reach the house after experiencing the smell and bustle of the yard.

The next chapter will examine the buildings of prosperous farmers and the continued differences between highland and lowland areas.

6
Marketing and Regional Buildings

THE wealth of English farmers increased greatly between 1500 and 1750, largely due to improvement in techniques – particularly grassland husbandry (see p. 17) – and the increased demand of urban markets, especially London. The incomes of many English yeomen probably doubled between 1500 and 1640, when grain prices increased more than sixfold, and the fall in grain prices after the 1640s Civil War benefited farmers in pastoral areas and encouraged more farmers in the south Midlands and parts of East Anglia to specialise in fattening cattle for market. Thus the open fields of the parish of Great Linford, Buckinghamshire, were enclosed in 1658 by butchers and graziers fattening cattle for the London market.

These developments provided farmers with the surplus cash to rebuild, and there is much evidence for the building of large farmsteads in this period. The 'large new frame of buildings' built on the estate farm of Buttas Manor in King's Pyon and Canon's Pyon, Herefordshire, in 1623 included a dairyhouse, kilnhouse, malthouse, stable, tiled barn, large barn, beasthouse, sheepcote, swinehouse and stone dovecote. A parsonage farmstead at St Michael Caerhays, Cornwall, de-scribed in 1680, had two courtyards with a malthouse, stable, two pigsties, oxhouse and threshing barn. The farm of a Devon yeoman, Thomas Blampin (died 1622), had a hen-house, cider house, corn barns, hay in 'lynney' and 'tallets' and an ox-house with great and little stalls 'for kyne'. Great Huxhill Farm in Weare Giffard, north Devon, has a large early seventeenth-century farmhouse, an L-shaped range of barns and stables, a cowhouse, granary and hay barn with cowhouse built in the seventeenth and early eighteenth centuries in dispersed fashion around a yard. Many farmsteads were rebuilt on the limestone belt, and also in Cumbria and the Yorkshire Dales, which testified to the wealth and new-found freehold status of upland farming, especially after the Civil War. In Northumberland, however, the prevalence of cattle rustling and local disorder retarded development until the later eighteenth century (see pp. 119–20): bastle houses, strong defensible buildings of stone where the farmer and his family lived above their animals, were not built after the Civil War but continued in use until much later.

Cheese, Beer and Cider

These large ranges of buildings demonstrated an increasing tendency on the part of many farmers to market their produce. South Cheshire and the Vale of Gloucester, for example, were exporting much dairy produce by the late sixteenth century. Three-storey dairies can be found from the eighteenth century in the Vale of Gloucester: after 48 hours in the cheese press, the cheeses were taken up steps or through a hatch to the shelf room, and after turning taken up to the cheese room, which had its wooden floor rubbed with fresh herbs every fortnight. The cheeses were packed in green leaves and then taken to market. John Francombe of Almonsbury left 7,100 cheeses when he died in 1716.

Much beer and cider would have been made on the farm, for they were popular elements in farmworkers' pay and the horn mug or wooden harvest

40. *Oast House, Brook, Kent, built 1815*
The circular plan kiln, with its distinctive conical roof, was invented by John Reade, a well-known gardener, and used from 1815 in Kent and 1835 in Herefordshire. Dried hops were unloaded from the drying floor of the kiln onto the first-floor cooling room of the attached weatherboard building. Photograph courtesy of Canterbury College of Art. The cowl was blown off during the savage gales of October 1987.

bottle were his (or her) constant companion. In 1695 Gregory King estimated that ale and beer amounted to 27.6 per cent and bread and corn only 20.5 per cent of annual household expenditure. Farm work was long (often from dawn to dusk in summer) and exhausting: Richard Jeffries, in *Hodge and His Masters*, 1880, wrote that 'Two gallons a day is a most common consumption with men who swing the scythe or reaping hook' and William Marshall,

85

writing of West Country farmworkers in 1789, disapproved of their low wages but 'exorbitant' drink allowances which would commonly exceed two gallons – 'drinking a gallon bottle full at a draught is said to be no uncommon feat'.

Many farmers, especially wealthier corn growers, had brewing equipment in their backhouses (attached to the back of farmhouses) or malthouses. East Anglia sent the greatest quantity of malted barley to London and abroad (malted barley was sent via Amsterdam to central Europe) and before the onset of scientific and industrial brewing in the nineteenth century the farmyard malthouse was a common sight.

The barley (oats and even beans were occasionally added) was steeped in a cistern of water for at least two days: plenty of floor space was needed for the next operation, when the barley was left to germinate on a timber or lime plaster floor; once the grain sprouted the malted grain was dried or heated on a kiln floor of brick or tile. The malt was then ground, mashed and brewed to make beer.

In the late sixteenth century the practice spread of adding hops to the brew for their preservative and flavouring qualities, and the government brought hop growers from the Low Countries to instruct farmers in their use. Hops were cultivated in many areas, but by the eighteenth century the commercial market had been cornered by Kent, Hereford and Worcestershire, mostly in anciently enclosed areas which had plenty of wood for hop-poles: by 1730, Kent – the nearest to London – accounted for 48 per cent of the hop trade.

Before being used, moist, freshly picked hops needed to be dried out. Reynolde Scot, in *A Perfect Platform for a Hop Garden*, 1574, wrote that they could be left to dry in the loft of a house for two or three weeks, but also recommended that they could be quickly dried over kilns in oast houses. The fire (usually of charcoal or anthracite) burned in a kiln, often with pans of sulphur which added colour and bitterness to the hops; the hot air then dried the hops, which were placed on hair cloths on a slatted floor in an upper room and turned over at regular intervals; outside steps enabled the workers to reach the drying floor easily. After about twelve hours they were raked out of the kiln, left to cool down on the cooling-house floor and then shovelled into long bags (called pockets) which were let into the floor; mechanical presses had been introduced in the mid-nineteenth century but usually the 'bagster' could have the unsavoury task of treading the hops in the bag whilst they were shovelled over him.

Essential to kiln design was mastery of the air flow and hence greater cost efficiency. An inverted pyramid, of lath and plaster in seventeenth-century examples, but of brick later, conducted the hot air from the kiln to the drying floor. The pyramidal roof was surmounted from the late eighteenth century by a cowl which turned downwind and so increased the flow of air. Circular kilns with conical roofs were introduced in the early nineteenth century but by the late nineteenth century a return to square kilns was accompanied by the invention of rollers to which drying cloths were fixed; a turn of the roller would safely deposit a load of hops onto the cooling floor. By the 1920s, the introduction of fans and oil firing had led to different types of kiln.

Hops, like the Mediterranean olive, demanded great investment of capital and labour – in hop poles (2–3,600 per acre), harvesting and drying, fuel and manure: Peter Bowden (in Thirsk (ed.), 1985) has estimated that hops cost five times more per acre to cultivate than corn. Invariably, the seventeenth-century kiln might be found at the end of a barn, now marked by different floor levels, but the survival from the eighteenth century of substantial numbers of oast-houses testifies to the high levels of capital necessary if commercial enterprise were to be viable. Indeed, in the 1730s and 1740s the increase of beer drinking made possible by the low price of corn encouraged farmers to boost production. From the later eighteenth century multiple complexes of oast-houses, such as the six square kilns at Sissinghurst Castle in Kent, were built by farmers to supply the increased demands of the London market.

By the Elizabethan age, the West Country had become famous for its cider, made from apples, and perry, made from pears. John Gerard, in his *Herball* of 1597, noted that around Hereford 'the servants drink for the most part no other drinke but that which is made from apples'. The Civil War spurred commercial production, and the period between 1650 and 1700 saw some orchards treble in size: fruit

trees were also grown in hedges, and by 1691 Celia Fiennes noted that Herefordshire was 'a Country of Gardens and Orchards'. The same period saw the coastal export of cider to London and the colonies: the building and extension of inland waterways from the late eighteenth century opened up new markets.

The areas which specialised in cider-making were Hereford and Worcester, Somerset, Devon, west Gloucestershire and south-east Wales. The process involved crushing the whole fruit to a 'pomage': the apples could be thrown into a barrel and mashed up by pounding with a pestle, but by the seventeenth

41. *Cider mill at Tarrington, near Hereford* Apples in the trough (chace) are mashed into a 'pomage' by the wheel, which has an axle attached to the horse-gear and cogged wheels to prevent the wheel from sliding when the trough is full. Note the press in the foreground. Photograph courtesy of the Museum of Cider, Hereford.

century the cider mill had been introduced. After crushing in the mill the pomage of mashed apples (called a 'cheese') was packed between layers of straw (in the south-west) or mostly in muslin cloths: it was then placed in an oak-framed press, whence the juice flowed into a stone trough. In some areas presses were not used and the weight of the pomage, stacked like a pyramid, forced the juice out. The dry residue might be fed to pigs or reground with water to make small cider. After a few days of fermenting in casks, the cider was put into fresh casks – this process being repeated for high-quality drink. It could be coloured with elderberries, burnt sugar or even sheep and cow blood.

To accommodate this equipment one would need a mill house, which in Marshall's words was 'as necessary as a barn in orchard country', although it might be no more than a 'mean shed or hovel, without peculiarity of form or any trace of contrivance'. The cider room, distinguished by its large and wide doorway, can be found in the service end of the house, at the end of a barn, under a granary or under a hop room. Few detached cider mills have survived: those that have generally date from the nineteenth century and are of good quality, having fruit lofts with trap doors to the mill. Large farmhouse cellars stored the produce away from frost.

Horn and Corn

The variety of underlying geology meant that some areas practising different forms of agriculture lay next to each other. A brilliant study of Chailey, East Chiltington and Falmer in East Sussex has shown the great difference that existed between the downlands of Falmer where large barns and shelter sheds stored corn and sheltered fatstock producing manure, and the adjoining wooded Wealden parishes where large numbers of cowhouses and yards reflect the importance of cattle breeding and fattening. The medieval fourteen-bay barn at Falmer Court set the pace, for barns in this former open-field parish are of at least five bays and of flint, contrasting with the mostly seventeenth-century weatherboard barns of Chailey and East Chiltington which are generally no more than five bays long. In 1842 the average size of a Falmer farm was 328 acres (131 hectares), contrasting with 86 and 96 acres (34 and 38 hectares) for the other parishes.

Arable farming encouraged the growth of large capital farms, which on the downlands of southern England or East Anglia would comprise at least 200 acres (80 hectares) and include large barns, yards and shelter sheds. The larger the farm, the less the unit cost reckoned in labour, plough teams and equipment. On pastoral farms, the keeping of dairy cattle encouraged closer supervision on the part of the owner and thus small farms with cowhouses. By 1600, for example, the sheep and corn farmers of the north Kent downs had at least 100 acres (40 hectares) of arable each but the average farm in the Kentish Weald would have had no more than 10 acres (4 hectares); in Wiltshire the farms of the southern downlands grew steadily larger as they specialised in growing more corn, but in the north of the county the increase of dairy farming encouraged small-scale family farms and even the sub-division of some large farms into smaller holdings. A similar contrast existed between the northern corn lands of Norfolk, with its large barns, great cartshed ranges and shelter sheds, and the dairying south and centre of Norfolk.

Norfolk, Essex and north Kent were the chief counties that exported corn and especially malt by river and sea to London. For example, there are four seventeenth-century barns at The

Grange, Takeley, Essex. William Marshall, in 1787, remarked that many Norfolk barns had no less than three threshing floors and were 'superior to those of every county'. The Broads area has the only aisled barns in Norfolk, notably at Hemsby and Rollesby.

Transport of produce by water was one-fifth the cost of carrying goods by land. As early as 1571, the River Lea was deepened as far as Ware in Hertfordshire so that corn and malt could be exported to London. In Oxfordshire, the River Cherwell was not navigable to Banbury and so its surrounding area, although blessed with good corn soils, became characterised by small dairy farms. In contrast, the country flanking the Thames from Oxford to Henley boasts many large barns which stored corn ready to be threshed and sent by barge to London. In the early seven-

42. *Bathampton Farm, Wylye, Wiltshire*
This farmstead, photographed in about 1930 and surrounded by Salisbury Plain, was typical of the southern English downlands. Note the corn ricks behind the barn, which has weatherboarded walls, and the dew pond in the foreground. Other walls are made of cob, and enclose a yard with shelter sheds which housed about 40 cattle producing manure for the surrounding fields. Photograph courtesy of the Institute of Agricultural History and Museum of English Rural Life, University of Reading.

teenth century Robert Loder of Harwell was one of many farmers who improved his lands and grew wheat and barley for export to London: wheat stored in his barn was gradually threshed and sold to Henley merchants between December and July. Many farms in this area have seven-bay barns with two threshing floors. At Chalgrove and Stonor late sixteenth-century five-bay barns were extended to nine bays in the early eighteenth century; at Britwell Salome, two five-bay aisled barns are dated 1743 and 1758. The aisled barns at Ipsden (built about 1756 and of 25 bays) and Preston Crowmarsh, Benson (20 bays, with 4 porches) are the largest in Oxfordshire and amongst the greatest in England.

Much of Wales was hampered by poor arable soil and bad communications, and barns greater than five bays are found only in the eastern lowlands (especially Montgomeryshire) and on the island of Anglesey, which boasts one of the largest barns in Wales at Henblas, dated 1733. Anglesey, blessed by several important estates, exported corn to many Irish Sea ports, including Dublin and Liverpool: the tenant on the farm at Fronddu, which faces Cemlyn Bay and has an eighteenth-century barn, kept vessels for this purpose.

In the cruck-building regions of the north and west Midlands and Welsh Borders, prosperous mixed farming had given rise to the creation of many large (over 150 or 200 acre, 60 or 80 hectares) farms and the building of many timber-framed or stone barns from the late sixteenth century. A survey of Radnorshire has noted the transition from the three-bay barn typical of the sixteenth-century farm to the seventeenth-century five-bay barn. Such barns, of at least five bays, replaced the three-bay cruck barns recorded on manor court rolls of the fourteenth and fifteenth centuries, although some medieval full-cruck four-bay

43a. *Farmstead at Stonor, Oxfordshire* Typical of the Henley/Oxford area: the barns, which date between about 1660 and 1720, and the eighteenth-century shelter shed form an L-shape which protects cattle from cold winds.

43b. *Wall End Barn, Great Langdale, Cumbria (left)* A small cruck barn (built 1612–15), typical of highland regions, where little corn was grown.

barns survive along the Welsh borders. Many barns, for example, were extended or built on the Dudmaston estate just south of Bridgnorth in Shropshire. Lye Hall barn, which dates from the late seventeenth century, was extended by four bays after Lye Hall was conveyed to the Wolryche family in 1725, and Quatt tithe barn was extended from seven to ten bays at this time. There are other seventeenth-century timber-framed five-bay barns at Lodge Farm and Little Holt and at Quatt Farm stands a five-bay stone barn described as 'newly built' in 1723.

As the economy became more market orientated the wetter and cooler areas of northern and western Britain specialised more in dairying or breeding and fattening cattle and large barns were rarely built. In 1698, Roger North had noted that 'the thrift of landlords had not afforded barns', the late harvest and dampness of the crop encouraging the practice of storing it on raised floors (see fig. 46).

In Ulster, where a survey of County Armagh in about 1820 showed that little more than a third of houses had barns attached, the usual practice was to store sheaves of corn in stacks which were gradually taken out and threshed in the open. William Marshall recorded in 1798 that oats – the staple crop of wetter climates – were threshed outside in Yorkshire and in the Vale of Pickering the annual outdoor rape threshing was a communal event.

Some wealthy farmers or landowners in highland areas continued to build cruck barns: Green Farm, Stocksbridge, Yorkshire, has a fifteenth-century aisled hall house and six-bay cruck barn, and sixteenth-century cruck barns lie next to Little Moreton Hall in Cheshire, Rivington Hall in Lancashire, and Deer How in Patterdale, Cumbria. The granary at Little Moreton lies within the gatehouse of the moated hall. However, cruck barns

of highland areas were mostly of three bays and rarely exceeded five bays in length. Peter Smith has drawn attention to the massive difference between a typical cruck barn of Merioneth with a storage capacity of 141 cu m (5,000 cu ft) and the typical aisled barn of the southern English downs which could hold 850 to 2266 cu m (30 to 80,000 cu ft). In 1599, a survey of Settrington in Yorkshire showed that all the houses and farm buildings were cruck-framed, and such structures continued to be built into the eighteenth century. Few have survived Victorian improvements and the evidence is fragmentary: for example, part of a scarfed cruck in a Bransdale cowhouse and the cruck-shaped gable wall of a cowhouse at Thoralby in Wensleydale, a feature found on other Dales buildings.

Carts or waggons were rarely used on hill farms. In Wales, the waggon was confined to the anglicised south and east and prosperous river valleys. Celia Fiennes, whilst making a tour of Devon and Cornwall in 1698, often met with teams of horses travelling nose to tail and carrying the harvest on frames: similar techniques prevailed in most upland areas until the beginning of this century. Sleds were used for harvesting hay or corn, and smaller sleds for transporting manure and lime. Dung was not taken to the fields by cart but in much smaller amounts by dung pots with opening bottoms which were carried on horseback. William Marshall made another important remark about upland farming when he wrote in 1798 that in Devon 'Twenty years ago, there was not a pair of wheels in the country, at least not upon a farm; and nearly the same may be said at present'. In the Yorkshire Dales there was usually no more accommodation than for one cart per farm, in complete contrast to the 'commodious' waggon sheds which Marshall noted in Norfolk: twelve-bay carthouses are still a common sight in northern Norfolk (see fig. 8). A survey of three parishes in East Sussex found that 88 per cent of cartsheds were on farms of over 100 acres, a size rarely exceeded on hill farms. Freestanding granaries, unknown in many highland areas, are found from the fifteenth century in Essex and other corn-processing parishes; the combined cartshed-granary building, found from about 1600 in Sussex and 1700 in north Norfolk (see fig. 8), was unknown in north-east Wales and other upland areas before the early 1800s (in Farndale, Yorkshire, the earliest cartshed is dated 1821).

With the abandonment of the long-house tradition more shelters were built to house cattle. One of these buildings was the 'linhay', a two-storey open-fronted building which had a hayloft placed over a cowhouse (see fig. 20). One of the earliest known examples is at Faenol Fawr in the Vale of Clywd, part of a late sixteenth-century gentry court-yard farm. Linhays are commonly found in the West Midlands, Hereford-shire, Cornwall and south Wales, but are especially common in Devon where many types of farm building are called linhay (such as cart-linhay). Their hay lofts were called 'tallets', as they were in south Wales, and were built with collars but no tie beams for ease of access.

The distribution of linhays is prob-ably significant, for they occur chiefly in the south of Devon, especially be-tween Churchstow and Averton Gif-ford, where fatstock were bred for their beef. Similarly, New Weston Farm at Bredwardine on the river Wye in Here-fordshire had a large twelve-bay barn 45.8 m (150 ft) long attached to a twelve-bay linhay built in about 1700 which probably housed fatstock pro-viding manure for the farm's arable. Dairy cattle, however, need better housing than beef cattle and enclosed cowhouses (such as those found in longhouses) are more common in high-er and wetter areas, for the linhay does not provide effective protection against driving rain. Indeed, the linhays on the Arlington estate in north Devon were all infilled with stone and made into cowhouses and other buildings in the mid-nineteenth century when the dairy industry was on the increase.

In northern England and north Wales, more severe winter weather meant that cattle needed to be housed indoors for up to twice as long as in the milder south-west; in the Yorkshire Dales, for example, cattle were not turned out until the last week of May. Consequently, shelter sheds are rare and buildings were built with as much as 75 per cent storage for hay and 25 per cent for the cattle thereby maintained. Many farms show evidence for the in-crease of cattle. A byre dated 1742 was added to a farmhouse at Martindale, Cumbria, and to the south in Lancashire and especially in Yorkshire many small cruck barns were built which had aisles for cattle, usually in a lean-to along one side. The greatest concentration of cruck barns, invariably of three to five bays, can be found in south-west York-shire and north Derbyshire – for example, in the parish of Bradfield, north-west of Sheffield. They are built of gritstone rubble with stone slate or Welsh slate roofs: each have through-entries with stone-flag threshing floors to one side and an entrance to a cow-house in a lean-to on the other side. The barn at Woodseats Farm, for example, may have been built in about the same year as the farmhouse, dated 1631. A similar four-bay cruck barn further to the north at Penistone is dated 1759.

Field barns which housed cattle and hay, mainly built without crucks, were used throughout Britain but especially in the Yorkshire Dales where they are now a distinctive feature. They were placed out in the fields so that they could receive hay from the surrounding meadow land, which was then con-sumed by cattle and strewn over the land as manure. James Tuke, writing in 1794, remarked that 'In the western dales, the cattle being housed in winter, haybarns, with a cow-house at one end and frequently at both, are placed on every three or four fields; by this means the hay and the manure are not carried any great distance; an important circumstance in these hilly countries and particularly so during the time of making hay in a country where the weather is very uncertain, attended with sudden frequent and violent showers. A farm of fifty or sixty acres will have five or six of these buildings'.

These field barns can be better understood as part of a specialised pastoral economy which produced dairy products, especially butter and the famous Wensleydale cheese, for export to the emergent industrial towns of the area. Partible inheritance had split holdings into small fragments by the seventeenth century. The average 15–20 acre (6–8 hectare) Wensleydale farmer had seven cattle on his farm in about 1700, and grazed sheep on the hills. In the North Riding, field barns are documented from the sixteenth century (many are mentioned in a 1614 survey of Wensleydale), but now all date from the enclosures of the decades around 1800. Each byre end would hold four or five cattle. They are most numerous in the parishes of Muker and Thwaite, at the head of Swaledale: here each farm has space for only a single cart and as early as 1631 a Muker farmer had 28 cattle, 2 horses, and 113 sheep but no corn at all. Larger field barns are more common to the south, starting in Wharfedale and Nidderdale but becoming general as one leaves the gritstone area and crosses into the more fertile limestone hills of the Craven Dales. They date from around 1700 and are characterised by large double doors in their side walls for unloading hay; each might accommodate more than 12 cattle. Inventories of the Craven area show that cattle at this time comprised 52 per cent of farm values. These cattle were fattened for the West Riding towns but some land was ploughed for corn which could be threshed out in the through-entries – which were given barn-like porches.

The mountainous landscapes of Snowdonia and Cumbria are also dotted with field barns for cattle; a few in the Lake District have threshing barns with cowhouses at the lower end. Some of these field barns have cruck trusses, suggesting seventeenth-century or even earlier dates. There are fewer examples than in the Yorkshire Dales, however, and only their lofts held hay. Most Welsh examples are long and low buildings for up to 12 cattle and adjoined hay barns or walled yards for haystacks. None were built after the mid-nineteenth century, by which time sheep had come to dominate mountain pastures. Many field barns in lowland

regions, such as the seventeenth-century timber-framed examples around Alcester in Warwickshire, were built only to house corn: some, such as in Dorset and the Cotswolds, have yards for winter housing of cattle and were evidently built to store hay.

By the late seventeenth century many highland farmers, having acquired virtual freehold status and enough capital, had dispensed with the cruck frame and built large farm buildings with king-post or tie-beam roofs. In Malham, North Yorkshire, where many barns with byres are dated around 1700, the barns and dovecote at Middle House east of Malham Tarn were built on the site of a Fountains Abbey shepherd's lodge. Nidderdale, further to the north, also has many farms on the sites of Fountains Abbey cattle lodges: a six-bay barn dated 1670 at Manor House has a byre at one end. Other wealthy

44. *Yorkshire field barns, Wensleydale* The typical field barn has accommodation for cattle at one or both ends, hay being stored in lofts above each byre and in two-thirds of the building's length. Armfuls of hay could be pulled from hatches in the partition wall out of the hay store (known as the 'sink mow') into the cow byre. These two barns, in Wensleydale, each have stalls for six cattle.

45. *Interior of barn at East Riddlesden Hall, Keighley, Yorkshire* One of two aisled barns built in about 1650 for James Murgatroyd, a Halifax clothier who rebuilt the Hall in 1648. Entrances in the gable end and inside the porches gave access to passages behind the cow stalls. The original mucking-out holes have been blocked up and the interiors of both barns have reset medieval stonework. Photograph courtesy of the Royal Commission on the Historical Monuments of England.

Dales farms have large (mostly five-bay) barns with byres and hay lofts at one or both ends. Thomas Preston built a fine farmstead arranged around a yard at Low Hall, Appletreewick, in 1690. His two barns each have byres entered from the side walls, storage in the centre for corn and hay and steps to lofts for storage or accommodation for farmhands. At Manor Farm, Threshfield, the barn dated 1661 has three doorways in the gable end giving access to a central feeding passage and flanking byres which hold up to twelve cattle (fig. 46.5). Similar barns with three gable doorways became very popular in Lancashire between 1750 and 1850.

Aisled barns in Yorkshire are almost all associated with the farms of great abbeys (such as Bolton) or later the wealthy gentry, such as the early fifteenth-century barn at Wadlands Hall. These barns are chiefly remarkable, however, in that many continued the tradition echoed in earlier cruck barns (such as Bradfield) by combining storage of corn with hay and livestock under wide and shallow-pitched stone slate roofs. Each barn at East Riddlesden Hall had stalls for over 40 head of cattle in the aisles, the hay probably being stored in the central nave. This arrangement was found in the Iron Age, for example at Ezinge in Holland, in the eighth century at St Gall monastery in Switzerland, and into the nineteenth century in parts of northern Europe: for example, the Dutch 'los hoes' farmhouse was an aisled building with the dwelling at one end and at the other the cattle and spinning rooms accommodated in aisles around a threshing floor and storage for hay (known as a haymow, as it was in Yorkshire).

Combination barns with floored ends for byres or stables are known from the medieval period – as at the Archbishop's Stables, Maidstone Palace, Kent, which is a barn with groom's lodging and stable at one end, Hales Barn (see fig. 34), the smaller barn of about 1400 at Swalcliffe, Oxfordshire, the early sixteenth-century nine-bay barn west of the Abbey church at Muchelney, Somerset, and the barn and stables built about 1485–9 by Sir Richard Edgcombe at Cotehele House in Cornwall. Barns with lofted ends for byres are known from the late sixteenth century in the Sussex Weald and West Midlands. In 1585, a parsonage farm at Binton, Warwickshire, had two three-bay barns, one being for hay 'wherein bestes be tyed'. Some sixteenth-century cruck barns in Devon were built on slopes with byres in two-storey lower ends, a feature known in Dorset, Cumbria and Derbyshire from the seventeenth century, Monmouthshire from the late sixteenth century, Radnorshire from 1713 and Denbighshire from 1677. Alternatively, the hay loft and byre could be fitted by lowering the barn floor at one end – as in the exceptionally fine seventeenth-century slatestone barn on a gentry farmstead at Pen-y-Bryn, Penmachno, Caernarvonshire. At Shroton, Dorset, a large late seventeenth-century U-shaped barn – adjoining a four-bay cartshed of the same date – has storage for hay and cowhouses in the wings flanking its rear yard. A feature of many barns in south-east England are the aisles for cowstalls

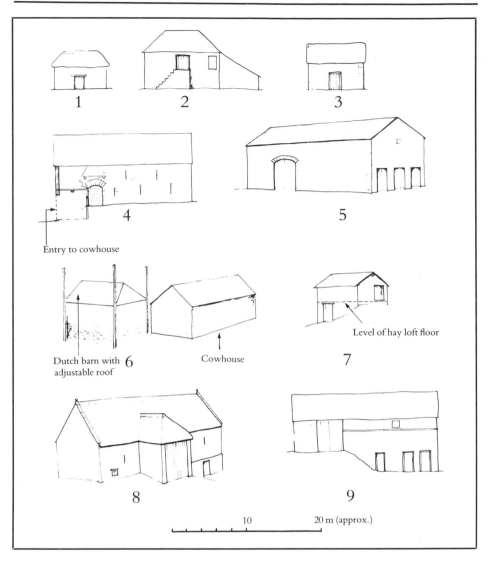

Entry to cowhouse

Level of hay loft floor

Dutch barn with 6
adjustable roof

Cowhouse

7

8

9

10   20 m (approx.)

46. Barns in highland areas were sometimes very small, or used to house cattle. (1) Eighteenth-century cob and thatch barn from mid Devon. (2) Early nineteenth-century two-level barn from east Cornwall, with threshing floor above cowhouse. (3) Seventeenth-century barn from North Yorkshire with heather thatching to roof (after Ingilby and Hartley, 1986). (4) Late seventeenth-century barn from Penmachno, Caernarvonshire, with hay loft and cowhouse to the left of the threshing floor doors.

(5) Barn with cowhouse (to right) at Threshfield, Wharfedale, Yorkshire, dated 1661. (6) Dutch barn and cowhouse of about 1830, south of Halifax, Yorkshire. (7) Early nineteenth-century Cumbrian hogg house (see p. 31). Early eighteenth-century barns, with cowhouses at their lower ends, from (8) Gorwell, Abbotsbury, Dorset, and (9) Troutbeck, Cumbria.

added on all sides, especially from the late seventeenth century: in the Rape of Hastings, for example, some barns had cattle housed at one end and were probably built to store hay.

The combination building *par excellence*, however, was the two-storey bank barn which provided storage for hay and corn with central threshing floor above byres, stables or other rooms. These are especially common in Cumbria and in the words of A. Pringle – reporter to the Board of Agriculture in 1805 – were 'frequently large enough to contain the whole crop of both corn and hay, so that it is rare to see a stack of either': the crop could be threshed and fed to the animals within the same building. The threshing barn, on the first floor, was entered by double doors approached from a raised bank. These banks could be artificially created: one can be seen in the heart of Borrowdale at Rosthwaite and there are other mid-nineteenth-century brick examples in the Solway Plain. The last bank barns were built just before the 1914–18 war, but their origins are obscure. Farm buildings which use hillsides to make easy access to dry and ventilated first-floor barns are found throughout the upland hills of Britain, also being found, for example, in Norway, the Dordogne in France, Umbria in Italy and Philadelphia in America.

In Cumbria, the oldest type of farm building is the conventional three or four-bay threshing barn, such as Wall End, Langdale, built 1612–15, or Low Hallgarth, Little Langdale (fig. 24). The bank barn had made its first appearance by the 1660s on farms of wealthy farmers, such as the Brownes of Troutbeck or the Flemings of Rydal Hall who bought Scottish drove cattle (often on credit) and fattened them over winter before sale in the spring. Sir Daniel Fleming, for example, housed 44 beasts in his 22 m (74 ft) long bank barn at Low Park besides lush pastures around Rydal

Water and the droving road to Ambleside, and another barn at Rydal Hall housed 28 cattle: in both examples the cattle faced the side walls, and backed onto a central manure passage, and this probably formed the original arrangement at another Fleming barn, 27.4 m (90 ft) long, at Coniston Hall and dated 1688. These were built by wealthy landowners in possession of good corn and meadow land, however, and most Cumbrian farmers in the period 1660–1749 had only eight or ten head of cattle which could be accommodated in a longhouse byre, and not until after this period did their numbers increase sufficiently to justify the building of bank barns, the great majority of which date between 1750 and 1860. The entrances, in the side walls, are usually shielded from driving rain by a canopy and in most instances give access to a cowhouse (usually for twelve cattle), stable and cartshed; some nineteenth-century examples have four-horse stables, root houses and feeding and dung passages to a 24-cow shippon. Lakeland farmers now made more money from the wintering and sale of cattle than the sale of wool. By the early nineteenth century the typical Lakeland farmstead might have one or more bank barns and other one-storey cowhouses.

Some particularly fine examples of bank barns can be found in Northumbria and south-west England. The eighteenth-century bank barn at Higher Churchill Farm, Arlington in north Devon, and early nineteenth-century example at Frogwell in Cornwall are in many respects identical to the Cumbrian model, and one of the finest English bank barns can be found near the river Tamar on the Launceston to Tavistock road. More typical of the south-west, however, is the two-level barn which uses steps rather than earth banks to reach the centrally placed door to the upper-level barn placed over a cowhouse. These are especially com-

mon on smaller farms in west Devon
and Cornwall and often have lean-tos
for cattle against one wall. The
Cotehele estate in Cornwall has many
examples of such two-level barns, with
central threshing floor over byres, dating from the late eighteenth century.
Such barns can also be found in north
Somerset, where J. Billingley considered them to be a recent introduction
in 1798 (fig. 46.2).

The limits imposed by climate, geology and topography, therefore, had
greatly influenced the appearance of our
farmsteads, but an equally important
factor, the continued development of
new techniques and large estates, shall
be the subject of the next chapter.

47. *Bank Barn, Townend Farm, Troutbeck, Cumbria* This fine barn stands opposite Townend Farmhouse which was owned by the prominent Browne family, for whom the barn was built in 1666. The ramp behind the tractor leads to the threshing floor of the main barn, which has an unusual extension for a winnowing floor to the rear, and stalls for cattle beneath. The 'Spinning Gallery' at the front leads to a plastered granary in the projecting wing on the left. Both features can be found in other large Lake District barns, such as Yew Tree Farm, Coniston. Photograph courtesy of The National Trust/David Pearson.

48. *Bank Barn at Broomhouses, Bellister, Northumberland, c. 1800 (left)*
The doors give access, from left, to a four-horse stable with loosebox, a cowhouse for twelve cattle, and a cartbay. The steps lead to a winnowing door and threshing floor on the first floor; the rear of the barn, which is set into a slope, has a wheel house (see p. 107) and hay barn. Cowhouses, a granary over a sheephouse and a house with labourer's accommodation were built at the same time, around a yard in front of the bank barn.

7
The Organised Farmstead

THE eighteenth century witnessed greatly increased efforts to boost agricultural production. The period of low corn prices to 1750, and especially the slump experienced by corn farmers after a spate of good harvests and low corn prices in the 1730s and 1740s, had certainly increased consumer demand and favoured pastoral farmers, but the main incentives to improve production came with the rising trend of prices between 1750 and 1813, as population grew from 5.7 million to over 10 million: this age of improvement has bequeathed us many of our finest farmsteads.

Four thousand Enclosure Acts were passed through Parliament between 1750 and 1850, bringing wasteland and the remaining open fields into more efficient methods of cultivation. The most active period of enclosure, between 1793 and 1815, was ushered in by a series of bad harvests and the onset of the Napoleonic Wars; corn immediately doubled in price and, in an effort to boost home production, corn fields again expanded onto marginal land – from chalk downland to upland moorland. In Kent, where the population doubled between 1750 and 1801, many flint barns and farm buildings were built on upper chalk downlands to serve new corn fields. On the coastal downs of Sussex, many farms with complexes of large barns were built in this period. The Great Forest of Brecon in Wales was enclosed between 1815 and 1818, as was much northern English moorland. When John Hutton enclosed Marske Moor in Swaledale in 1810 he built a new 800 acre (320 hectare) farm 1,100 ft above sea level. Cordilleras Farm, as it was called, exhibited all the features of a pioneering settlement, with new roads, walls and drainage: holes were bored for water pipes which led to the farmstead.

The ruins of new limekilns bear witness to the improvement of acidic soils for growing corn in this period, such as those built in the 1820s along the River Torridge, south of Bideford in Devon for Lord Rolle, who imported limestone from the Gower Peninsula and Caldy Island in south Wales.

After Napoleon's defeat at Waterloo in 1815 prices returned to normal and the easy credit boom ended. Corn prices fell and arable farmers – especially on marginal and badly drained soils – were forced to reduce their arable acreages (Cordilleras Farm had become pastoral by the 1830s). In many areas a farming slump, aggravated by social tensions as rural unemployment soared in the south, persisted into the 1830s. Thus plenty had bred poverty and British farmers suffered from their own success.

Improved Techniques

Increases in productivity were accompanied by attempts to improve and standardise the farmyard plan. The courtyard plan, with barn to north of cowhouses and yards which faced south to catch the sun, became the most common type of plan on farms of over 200 acres. Enclosure facilitated the erection of courtyard farms on new sites. In Northamptonshire, William Pitt noted that 'old farmsteads were pent up in villages and are consequently either on one side of the farm or totally detached and off from it', and in Staffordshire noted that they were 'without design or contrivance'. The difference is clearly apparent in some areas, for example in Oxfordshire: thus a pre-improvement farmstead on Boar's Hill near Oxford, dating from 1699, has a dispersed layout of buildings but a farm in Eynsham, which was enclosed in 1802, is typical of improved designs by having its farmhouse facing away from its buildings, which are built around a quadrangular yard (see fig. 3).

More flexible rotations, new fodder crops (especially turnips) and improvements in grassland husbandry resulting in more winter hay not only facilitated the keeping of more cattle over winter but also led to an increase in their average size, and yields. In the thirteenth century Walter of Henley estimated a good cow's annual yield at 98 lb (44 kg) of cheese and 14 lb (6 kg) of butter, but Vancouver in 1813 put the average cow's yield at 140 lb (63 kg) of cheese and 206 lb (93 kg) of butter. Archaeological evidence suggests that most cattle up to the fifteenth century were only 1.2 m (4 ft) high at the shoulder but thereafter showed an increase to about 1.5 m (5 ft) (the size of a modern Jersey heifer). Between 1710 and 1795 the cattle weighed in at Smithfield market showed a remarkable increase in average weight from 370 lb to 800 lb. There were many breeds of cattle. Most notably, Robert Bakewell of Dishley in Leicestershire was a famous breeder of Longhorn cattle and in the early 1800s breeders such as Robert and James Colling of County Durham perfected the Shorthorn breed. The Shorthorn was favoured as a dual-purpose dairy/beef cow and by the mid-nineteenth century separate dairy and beef strains had been developed. These improvers favoured a massive form on spindly legs. The Craven Heifer, portrayed on etchings and paintings in many farmhouse parlours, was such a massive beast that the doorway to its cowhouse (formerly a barn) on the Bolton Abbey estate in Yorkshire had to be increased to 1.5 m (5 ft) wide.

Turnip farming had originated amongst the East Anglian gentry in the seventeenth century, when this area imported a large, and increasing, number of Scottish and Welsh cattle for fattening on crushed grains, root crops, beans and other products such as oil cake. Between 1650 and 1750 the average Lincolnshire farm saw its numbers of fattening cattle increase to 19 whilst its numbers of dairy cattle decreased from 6.7 to 4. Defoe, in the 1720s, mentioned the great numbers of Scots and Welsh cattle fattened on Midland and East Anglian pastures. The first shelter shed in lowland Staffordshire dates from 1754, by which time fold yards were given over to fatstock. In 1798 William Marshall found intensive stall feeding in the Vale of Gloucester. Herefordshire bullocks, fed on hay, corn, oilcake and linseed, were accommodated in special houses which had mostly been built since the 1770s: each building had a root house opening onto a range of pens each with its own yard. The bullocks, once fattened, were sent 100 miles to Smithfield market.

In many areas, cattle were first fattened on fattening grounds near the house: as winter set in and hooves threatened to pound pasture into mud, they were moved to yards where they were fed on hay and root crops. Cattle choke on large pieces of food, and so new machines for chopping up turnips and straw appeared on the market from the 1760s, followed by the introduction of fodder rooms from the 1770s and boilers for fodder from the 1790s. New cowhouses were built with the cattle standing across the building and facing the feeding passage; William Marshall found in 1798 that new courtyard farms in Yorkshire had this arrangement, although some farmers continued to build narrow 'hovels' which made this arrangement impossible. Cattle could also be fattened in yards, hammels or looseboxes. Courtyard farms were also ideally suited to the efficient production of manure, which was kept in the foldyard or dungpit and then forked into carts and spread over the fields to continue the farming process: 'Muck is the mother of moncy' ran the old Norfolk proverb. Bailey and Culley noted in 1805 that October saw many Northumbrian farmers house their cattle and feed them on turnips and bran: 'In some parts of this country, where the turnip culture is carried to such extent, every exertion of ingenuity is practised to

raise a large portion of farm-yard dung'. From the late eighteenth century we find more and more examples of outfarms for the production of manure – these have shelter sheds for cattle (sometimes sheep) flanking a yard and barn.

The increasing desire to make organised and interlinked layouts was reflected in the farmstead designs printed in numerous pattern books from the 1740s. William Halfpenny, a champion of chinoiserie, published his *Twelve Beautiful Designs for Farmhouses* in 1750. The buildings are arranged around yards but show no marked regard for the economy of labour, the barns often

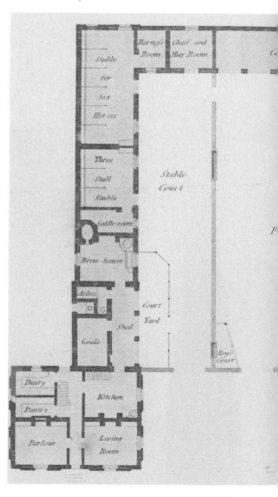

49. *Plan of model farm illustrated in C. Waistell's* Designs for Agricultural Buildings, *1827. Corn from the rickyard was conveyed to the barn where it was made into grain and straw. Straw was then taken to the cattle. Young stock needed the most straw, and were therefore placed in yards nearest the barn; horses were positioned furthest from the barn because they needed the least straw. Note also the isolated position of the cartshed, thus keeping the stock yards clear of traffic.*

lying at the furthest possible distance from the cowhouse. Daniel Garret's *Designs and Estimates of Farmhouses for the County of York etc*, 1747, shows a more thoughtful approach: for example, in one plan, the stock yard lies to the south of a barn, flanked by cattle sheds which face a foldyard; the pigsties are placed near to the dairy. A plan by R. Lugar of 1807, however, shows the barn separated from the cowshed and the pigsties more than a hundred-foot walk from the dairy. C. Waistell's posthumous *Designs for Agricultural Buildings*, 1827, is eminently practical and interlinked elements in each plan show a thorough awareness of the functions of an improved farmstead.

From the 1770s threshing machines appeared which sought to mechanise the threshing process and were quickly accepted in some areas. The most suc-

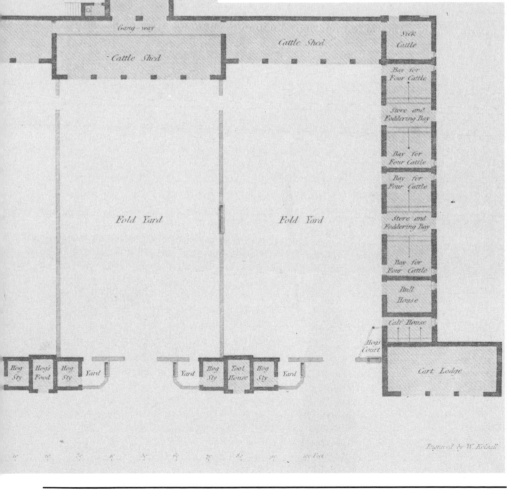

cessful design was by Andrew Meikle of East Lothian in 1786. The unthreshed sheaves of straw were fed through rollers into a revolving drum fitted with pegs which threshed out the grain, the grain fell into a box beneath and the straw was taken out by rollers. In later versions shakers shook out any grains left on the straw and winnowing fans completed the process.

There were various ways of providing power to work threshing machines. Thus water wheels were placed alongside barns and even windmills on barns in exposed places, particularly in the north-east: one can be seen on a farmstead at Chollerton, Northumberland. Horsepower was the most popular: distinctive wheel houses, instantly recognisable, were built to shelter horses which pulled great overhead crown wheels providing power to barn machinery and even cider mills.

Beans and corn still might be threshed out by hand, but machine threshing was so much quicker that the corn was now mainly stored in ricks and the barn became a smaller building mainly for the storage of straw: the rick yard could hold ten times as much corn as the barn. Agricultural writers recommended rickyards and condemned large barns as wasteful.

Contemporary observers considered that the installation of a threshing machine (which would cost over £100 as against £10 for a plough) would be cost effective only if the farm had enough land for two or three ploughs, or 100–150 acres. Another important factor, apart from farm size, was the expense of labour. Many threshing machines were installed during the Napoleonic Wars, as wage rates and corn prices rose, and in Northumberland and Durham many farms with wheel houses for threshing machines can be found above the 500 ft mark on marginal land tilled in the early 1800s. Most wheel houses can be found in the north-east, where wage rates were very high due to competition from local industry, and from the late 1780s farmers installed threshing machines mostly on dry loam soils suited for turnip husbandry. In 1805 Bailey and Culley estimated that the Northumbrian farmer would have to pay 26s for threshing out

264 bushels (approximately 9,000 litres) of grain as against only 1s 6d if machine threshed.

The fertile Vale of York, particularly around Sessay, south of Thirsk, and Holderness provide plentiful examples in contrast to the pastoral Dales. In the East Yorkshire Wolds courtyard farmsteads were built from the mid-eighteenth century as Enclosure Acts converted great tracts of common pasture to arable land, and threshing machines, according to Strickland, were 'becoming very general on the considerable farms throughout the district' by the early 1800s. Most examples in Shropshire, Cornwall and north Wales date from the years of arable expansion between the late 1790s and 1820.

In much of East Anglia and southern England, however, wage rates were much lower and threshing machines correspondingly few in number. The mowing of wheat had also been introduced as a labour-saving device in 1771, but hand threshing in other areas remained an essential source of winter income for the rural poor. After 1815, when war ceased and the farming depression set in, many farmworkers, haunted by fears of unemployment, burned ricks and smashed threshing machines. In Norfolk, where machines had been introduced in 1805, a Mendham rioter of 1822 testified that 'the general sense of the country was in favour of putting a final stop to machinery of every kind', and during the famous Jack Swing riots of the 1830s farmers often left their threshing machines out as targets in the hope that their farm buildings would be saved.

Estates and the Growth of Large Farms

The courtyard farm was rarely built on farms of under 150 acres, and is therefore a reflection of the increased size of farms. When Arthur Young wrote that 'Great Farms are the Soul of Norfolk culture', he must have been thinking of the county's cornlands where most farms, built around yards, exceeded 300 acres. The low corn prices and rising land values of the early eighteenth

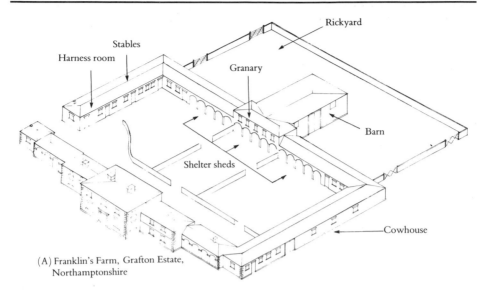

(A) Franklin's Farm, Grafton Estate, Northamptonshire

51. *(A) Perspective Plan of about 1832, of Franklins Farm, Grafton Estate, Northampton-shire* This served a farm of 400 acres, and was one of the model farms designed by the land agent John Green for the Duke of Grafton. Note the position of the barn, which antici-pates the steam-powered Victorian mill barn (see fig. 57). The layouts at Robinson's Farm (B) and Dunckley's Farm (C) served smaller farms. Courtesy of The Duke of Grafton and Northamptonshire Record Office.

century encouraged many small far-mers to abandon the risks of a hard-won living and enjoy the relative security of an improving landlord. En-closure, by forcing farmers to face the uncertainties of the market place alone and without the support of communal regulation, was another factor in the growth of large farms. Larger farmers, moreover, had the capital to invest in building new farm buildings, in drain-age and other improvements.

A study of the lower Ouse Valley between 1780 and 1840 has revealed the expansion of family estates, the purchase of smallholders' estates by landlords and wealthy rentiers and the resulting replanning of fields and re-location of farmsteads: by 1840 over 90 per cent of the valley was owned by 30 people, including 50 per cent owned by only 5 families with farms exceeding 1,000 acres. By 1851 large farms of over 300 acres (120 hectares) comprised one-third and the landlord-tenant sys-tem about 80 per cent of England's cultivated acreage, especially in low-lying arable areas where the higher unit cost of growing corn had forced many small farmers out of business. The landed interest still dominated Parlia-ment in 1872, when four-fifths of the country was owned by only 7,000 peo-ple.

Generally, a landlord needed to spend not less than 4 per cent of his gross rental on repairs and improve-ments if his lands were not to fall into decay. Farm buildings comprised a fraction of this expenditure. Between 1790 and 1815 half of the expense on enclosures on the Fitzwilliam estates in Northamptonshire and Huntingdon-shire went on hedging and fencing, and only one-sixth on farm buildings.

Estates often ploughed about 10 per

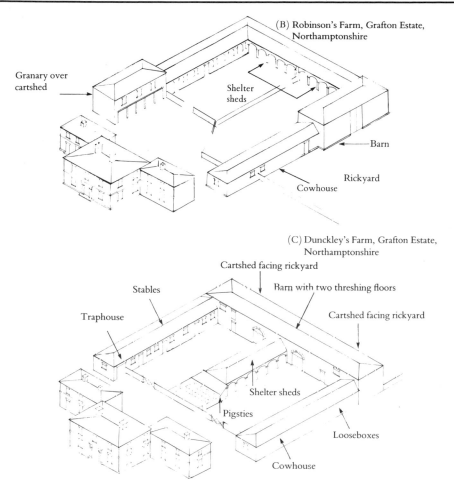

(B) Robinson's Farm, Grafton Estate, Northamptonshire

Granary over cartshed

Shelter sheds

Barn

Rickyard

Cowhouse

(C) Dunckley's Farm, Grafton Estate, Northamptonshire

Cartshed facing rickyard

Stables

Barn with two threshing floors

Traphouse

Cartshed facing rickyard

Shelter sheds

Pigsties

Looseboxes

Cowhouse

cent of their gross rentals back into land and as rentals rose (they more than doubled between 1750 and 1790) the incentive to invest increased – with a likely rate of return of anything between 6 and 12 per cent per annum. Traditionally, landlords would provide tenants with the fixed capital for buildings and land improvement, whilst the tenant provided the working capital such as seeds and implements. The landlord recognised that such investment would keep or attract good tenants. In 1765 a surveyor of the Grafton estates in Northamptonshire noted that if a good tenant had a farmyard of

bad buildings his lordship should repair them. The monument to Sir Thomas Parkyns in the church at Bunny, Nottinghamshire, records that he rebuilt many of the farms on his estate 'Contriving & Drawing all the Plannes without an architect'. Many of his brick farm buildings survive, with his initials and dates (between 1719 and 1736) made of black header bricks, as well as the school and almshouse he built in 1700, and Bunny Hall in 1723.

In the eighteenth century leasehold tenure continued to increase in popularity and landlords often inserted clauses enjoining their tenants to farm in progressive ways. In 1739 one land agent wrote to his lord that 'in future a covenant to oblige tenants to maintain their buildings will be worth while': by 1800 such covenants had become usual practice. This had been recognised since medieval times, because landlords had frequently ordered tenants to carry out repairs to their farm buildings and often supplied sufficient timber for the purpose. In the seventeenth century, the Flemings of Rydal Hall, Cumbria, and the Myddletons of the Ruthin Castle Estate in Wales were typical of many seventeenth-century landlords in repaying tenants who had carried out their own repairs – it was not until 1875 that such compensation was made compulsory. The Lincolnshire custom of tenant right, whereby tenants were compensated for their improvements upon leaving their farms, was much praised by contemporaries.

English farm tenants now enjoyed the best farming conditions in the world. Land agents, who often drew up plans for farm buildings (see figs. 51 and 52), had played an increasingly large part in managing estates and some achieved national prominence, such as the Scotsmen Francis Blaikie and James Loch. James Loch (who became notorious through his work on the Highland Clearances with the Duke of Sutherland) made remarkable improvements on the Marquess of Stafford's estates and, with the steward William Lewis and architect John Smith, rebuilt the farmsteads on the Lilleshall and Trentham Estates in Shropshire and Staffordshire between 1811 and 1820. The Yarborough estate in Lincolnshire had five brickyards in the 1830s, and the Duke of Northumberland's Alnwick estate was typical of other vast estates in that it had its own works department and building surveyor. In England the landlord, therefore, had a keen interest in farming matters, in contrast to parts of the Continent where the landlord-tenant system did not exist and landlords contentedly remained absentee rentiers. Thus Arthur Young, after a visit to France, had written that 'Banishment alone will force the French to execute what the English do for pleasure – reside upon and adorn their estates'.

A curious manifestion of this interest in agriculture was the decorative farmstead, or *'ferme ornée'*, invariably built by a leading architect of the day. William Kent built two cowhouses with classical arches and castellated parapets in his wonderful classical park of the 1730s at Rousham, Oxfordshire. The most dramatic group of Gothic-style farm buildings was designed by Thomas Wright, a former astronomer, for the fourth and fifth Dukes of Beaufort at Badminton in Gloucestershire: the massive Castle Barn is battlemented like Rousham, but its dramatic form is influenced by the Baroque medievalism of Vanbrugh. Charles, eleventh Duke of Norfolk, erected similar farmsteads on the land enclosed in 1778 on his Greystoke Castle estate in Cumberland. The Duke named his fanciful farmsteads after rebel generals and victories in the American War of Independence in order to spite Lord Lonsdale, his Tory neighbour and hated political rival.

52. *Lilleshall Hill Farm, Shropshire*
h = men's room over brewhouse; e = dairy; i = hackney stable; 2 = harness rooms; 3 = shelter shed; 4 = calf house; 5 = cowhouse; 6 = turnip room; 7 = working horses; 8 = granary over cartshed; 9 = tool house and grain store; 10 = barn; 11 = pigsties. This plan was published in James Loch's *Improvements on the Estates of the Marquess of Stafford*, 1820. The buildings, made of brick and tile except the timber-framed barn, were erected in 1818 and served a newly enclosed farm. Others of Loch's designs had buildings and a wide paved causeway surrounding a foldyard, and threshing machines powered by water wheels and even steam.

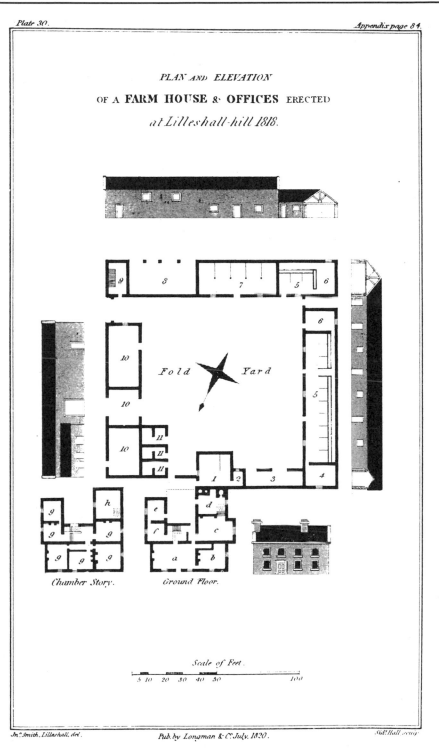

Plate 30.

Appendix page 84.

PLAN AND ELEVATION

OF A **FARM HOUSE & OFFICES** ERECTED

at Lilleshall-hill 1818.

Fold Yard

Chamber Story.

Ground Floor.

Scale of Feet.

5 10   20   30   40   50   100

Jn.º Smith, Lilleshall, del.

Pub. by Longman & Cº July, 1820.

Sd.º Hall sculp

The dairy, kept clean and fresh as protection against disease, was often chosen as an acceptable building for ladyfolk and visitors and built near the house as a symbol of purity and innocence. Marie Antoinette's dairies in Le Petit Trianon at Versailles are symptomatic of this paradoxical longing for a rural arcadia but seclusion from the everyday life and work of the land. Dairies were often octagonal and designed in Greek neo-classical style, such as Robert Adam's dairy at Croome Court, Worcestershire, 1760–73. James Wyatt built octagonal dairies at Belvoir Castle, Rutland, and Shugborough Park, Staffordshire, (see pp. 114–17) the latter based on the first century B.C. Tower of the Winds in Athens and fitted with Athenian-style dairy pots. The Duchess of Norfolk, a keen agriculturalist, kept a collection of books on farming in the dairy built about 1760 at her farm buildings at Worksop Manor, Nottinghamshire.

To followers of Rousseau and his philosophy of the 'Noble Savage' a primitive style of building was deemed a more fitting evocation of Nature: Philip Yorke (1757–1834), Third Earl of Hardwicke, commissioned Sir John Soane, the country's most highly original architect, to build 'a Dairy in the primitive manner of Building' at Hammels, Hertfordshire, as an anniversary present for his wife in 1793. Rustic simplicity also provided the inspiration for John Plaw in his book on *Ferme Ornée*, 1795, which has many designs for buildings with columns of tree trunks. Indeed, it was generally held that the design of the classical Greek Doric column had been derived from the tree trunk – Soane used simplified baseless Doric columns for the Hammels dairy and his barn 'à la Paestum' (after the classical temple in Sicily he visited in 1779) built in 1798 at Malvern Hall, Solihull. Despite these pretensions, 'primitive building' was too self-conscious to descend to the vernacular level, but Soane, son of a Berkshire builder, had sufficient grasp of local building styles to design a remarkable series of farm buildings for Philip Yorke's Home Farm in Wimpole in Cambridgeshire, built in 1794–6. Some of his designs, such as the dairy, dovecote and poultry yard were never executed and some – such as the piggery – have been demolished, but the deer pens, cartshed and granary and thatched barn survive. The present dairy was built in 1862. Soane designed other farm buildings such as the semicircular group of cowhouses at Burn Hall, County Durham, and a group at Port Eliot, Cornwall. The cowshed at Port Eliot is typical of Soane's functional approach to 'ferme ornée' for the fluted frieze beneath the eaves is a sliding ventilator.

Although delightful to the tourist and the modern eye, the 'ferme ornée' was regarded as foppish and impractical by many commentators. Other landowners took a more serious and productive interest in their estates. The Third Earl Spencer, for example, who bred cattle in looseboxes on his Home Farm at Wiseton from 1814, was an active politician, but during his term as

53. *Castle Barn, Badminton, Gloucestershire, c. 1750*
Thomas Wright, an architect and astronomer, designed several castellated barns and cowhouses for the Badminton estate. The towers and battlements hide the buildings to the rear: cartsheds are built into each tower, and a central seven-bay barn is flanked by yards for cattle and projects at right angles to the rear. Photograph by courtesy of *Country Life*.

Chancellor of the Exchequer it was said that each morning he opened his bailiff's letters and farm accounts before seeing to the affairs of State; the same story was told of Horace Walpole when he was Prime Minister. English businessmen were (and still are) noted for discarding their roots in trade or industry and assuming the mantle of the country squire. Thus Christopher Sykes, from a rich Hull trading and banking family, was made a baronet for his improvements of the Yorkshire Wolds. His mansion at Sledmere, begun in 1788, is decorated with a frieze depicting agricultural scenes and looks across the park to Castle Farm, built around 1778 by John Carr of York. Sykes designed most of his farmsteads.

New farming ideas were passed around with crusading zeal from the highest in the land. George III not only imported the Merino sheep from Spain in 1792 but also published articles in Arthur Young's *Annals of Agriculture* under the guise of his shepherd Ralph Robinson. Books were of some importance in influencing land agents and architects. Arthur Young's *Annals of Agriculture* by his own admission had a readership of around only 400, but J. C. Loudon's *Encyclopaedia of Agriculture* (crammed with new ideas for farm buildings) sold 9,000 copies between publication in 1825 and 1865. Ideas could be exchanged among a wider audience in the market place, local newspapers and, from the 1790s, local agricultural societies. Specially trained servants also spread ideas: thus in the 1720s turnips for fodder were introduced in and around Rock in Northumberland by gardeners imported for the purpose.

For experimenting farmers, such as the Egremonts of Petworth, the home farm became the centre of operations and a showpiece for visitors. The Earl of Raby's home farm of about 1755 at Darlington, County Durham, had a façade by James Paine in Gothic style and buildings set out by the Earl 'wherein every new erection for useful knowledge in husbandry and beneficial improvement in modern agriculture were practised', according to the county's historian William Hutchinson in 1794.

Samuel Wyatt (1737–1807) – who came from a farming family – was an extraordinarily able architect who designed all types of buildings, such as country houses, lighthouses, factories and farm buildings. Thomas William Coke (1754–1842), a leading agricultural improver who had inherited the Holkham Hall estate in Norfolk in 1776, employed Wyatt to design his farmsteads. Wyatt built three field barns on Coke's home park, which had been improved and extended to near 3,000 acres (1,200 hectares) by about 1790. Of these the Great Barn, finished in 1790, was the most famous and only rivalled in its splendour by James Paine's great barn with corner towers built in 1798 at Weston Park, Staffordshire. The Great Barn formed the setting for Coke's annual sheep shearings which became enlightened conferences on agricultural improvement with day tours and evening talks: the 1821 shearings, for example, were attended by 7,000 people. Young noted that 'the front edge of his [Wyatt's] mangers are rollers covered with tin; the mangers themselves are plated with iron; and the bottoms of the stall fences are of slate' from Penrhyn in north Wales, where another Wyatt, Benjamin, built slatestone farmsteads in his capacity as Lord Penrhyn's agent. Between 1790 and 1842 £1–3,000 was spent on each new Holkham farm, the plans usually consisting of a central barn for corn and fodder, surrounded by cowhouses.

Holkham's influence undoubtedly spread far and wide. Marshall commented that Midland farmers travelled great distances for new ideas: farm

54. *The Great Barn, Holkham, by Samuel Wyatt, 1790* A shrine of the Agricultural Revolution. Originally surrounded by cattle sheds, the Great Barn contains a central corn barn flanked by accommodation for cattle and horses, a threshing machine, granary and roothouses. Photograph courtesy of E. Swain.

buildings at Betley in Staffordshire were modelled on examples from Holkham. At Shugborough Park in Staffordshire a great flood in 1795 gave Thomas Anson, Coke's son-in-law, the chance to clear away the former field barns and village to the south of Shugborough Hall and create a massive home farm of 2,000 acres (800 hectares) served by the farm buildings at Whitebarn and Home Farm (now Shugborough Park Farm), by Samuel Wyatt. Whitebarn Farm consists of an east-facing cattle yard with a barn to the west. The barn has no threshing bay for it is one of the first barns to use water-power to drive its threshing machine (which was capable of threshing out 200 bushels, or approximately 7,000 litres, of grain each day). The stream continues in a channel over the railway to irrigate the kitchen garden and to meet the pond at Home Farm.

William Pitt, in his *General View of the Agriculture of Staffordshire*, 1805, wrote that Home Farm consisted of 'the farming steward's house at one end: a range of buildings along one side contains a brewhouse upon a large scale, a water corn-mill for the family and farm use and in which corn is ground for the neighbouring poor gratis, and a malthouse; the opposite side and end are occupied by stables and other appendages; and in the middle of the yard is a very complete hoggery, built of large

55a. *Barn at Whitebarn Farm (right)* This was one of the earliest barns built to house a threshing machine, and therefore has no conventional large barn doors.

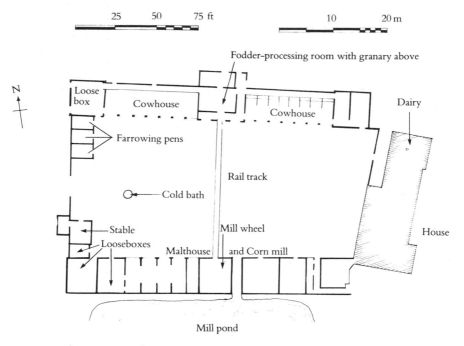

Fodder-processing room with granary above

25   50   75 ft   10   20 m

N

Loose box
Cowhouse
Cowhouse
Dairy

Farrowing pens

Cold bath

Rail track

Stable
Mill wheel
House
Looseboxes
Malthouse   and Corn mill

Mill pond

stones set edgeways, and covered with slate, with a boiler for heating hog feed, a cold bath supplied by the mill stream, for giving an occasional swill to the young pigs, and in which a number of hogs are fatted on dairy refuse, boiled roots or vegetables, pulse, ground barley or bran supplied by the mill near at hand'.

Livestock included 1,700 prize-winning Southdown sheep and 100 head of cattle including Longhorns improved by stock from Thomas Coke's herd at Holkham. These included about 30 dairy cows and in the 1804 season '60 head of cattle were stall-fed, entirely on the produce of the farm; they were all finished up at the same time, and the greater part sent to Smithfield'. Other improvements on the estate were noted by Pitt, such as the change from 20 draught oxen to 30 draught horses in 1784, the sowing of turnips in rows by drill and weeding by horse-hoeing. He noted that 250 acres (100 hectares) of meadow provided 'eleven very large stacks (of hay) . . . besides which there is

a very large quantity of old hay in hand'.

The estate was situated near two canals, convenient for exporting its produce and importing lime and fuel·£1,100 had been spent on the purchase of lime in one year. Cheeses, for example, were regularly exported from Weston Wharf down the Trent and Mersey Canal to Birmingham. The dairy produced 3–400 cheeses every year and 250–500 pounds (112.5–225 kg) of butter each month.

Primarily, however, Home Farm existed to provide the Ansons, their staff and guests at Shugborough Hall with plentiful supplies of food and drink. In August 1812, for example, the brewhouse supplied Shugborough Hall with 34 bushels (approximately 1,200 litres) of malt and the dairy great quantities of cream, milk, butter (158 lb or 71 kg) and cheese (106 lb or 48 kg); the farm also produced bread flour, veal (87 lb or 39 kg), 1,037 lb (467 kg) of meat, and 56 bushels (1,860 litres) of oats, 26 bushels of hay and 10.5 bushels of straw for the

riding and carriage horses. Home Farm was staffed by 22 labourers in 1805, as well as a man who managed the mill and malt house, who were supervised by the steward or bailiff, Mr Wheelock. The farm was leased out after 1828.

The fortunes of many farmsteads, therefore, reflected the fortunes of the estates who owned them. The Dudmaston estate, just south of Bridgnorth in Shropshire, went through its worst period of financial difficulty after the Civil War, reaching a nadir with a legacy of near bankruptcy, jointures and settlement left by the 'Wolryche Fool' after his death in 1722. After 1774, William Whitmore breathed new life into the estate, followed by his son William Wolryche Whitmore (born 1784). In 1776, £420 was spent on rebuilding the house, barn and stable at Lodge Farm. Between 1776 and 1816 the rental increased from £811 to £3,986 due to drainage and other improvements. The buildings were still in a sorry state and it was left to William Wolryche Whitmore from the 1830s to rebuild the

55b. Home Farm, Shugborough Park, Staffordshire The farmyard originally surrounded a hoggery. Only the pigs' cold bath now remains in the yard, which is transversed by an iron trackway for carrying milled corn from the mill to the granary which provided fodder to its adjoining cowhouses. The photograph shows the malthouse range to the south.

estate buildings in brick and tile from the Madeley Wood works, 20 miles to the north, which superseded the old materials of timber, thatch and crumbling sandstone. William Whitmore was a keen agriculturist, who conducted experiments, helped set up the Bridgnorth Agricultural Society and founded an Industrial School in Quatt, the estate village which he rebuilt in the 1840s.

The Attingham estate, just west of Shrewsbury, was built up after the acquisition of the park in 1700 by the Hill family, mostly between 1743 and 1808, to mark the family's ascent into the aristocracy. Noel Hill, who inherited the estate in 1782, knocked down Tern Hill

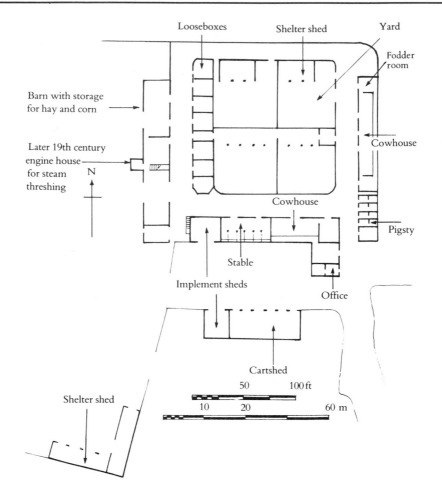

(a modest early Georgian mansion house) and began work on Attingham Hall in 1783, using the well-known James 'Athenian' Stuart as his architect. Hill was made a baronet in 1784. The farm buildings reflect the growth of the estate, starting with the barn with crow-stepped gables dated 1745 at Norton and similar-style stables and granary at Uckington. The pedimented stables flanking the farmhouse at Lower Betton and the fine classical stables at the outfarm at Berrington Buildings both suggest a 1780s date and the guiding hand of an architect such as Stuart. An 1808 map also shows buildings built around yards at Smethcott, Uckington and Duncot, most of the estate farms by now serving around 300 acres (120 hectares) each.

The home farm, which has a fifteenth-century farmhouse, was not acquired until 1777. The farm buildings were replanned in the 1850s, and include a slaughterhouse, which is a small building of 4.6 × 7.3 m (15 × 24 ft) with its stunning block and winch for hauling up carcasses still in place. The unfortunate beasts were kept in two adjoining fasting pens until their time came for slaughter; offal from the slaughter house and whey from the farmhouse dairy, close by, were fed to the pigs accommodated in two near-by

rows of sties. Such slaughterhouses were rarely built and only survive on large estates, especially near country houses – sources of so much conspicuous consumption. The farm at Cronkhill, behind the picturesque house built by Nash in about 1802 for Lord Berwick's Agent, is the most impressive group on the estate.

In Northumberland and Durham the scarcity of freeholders and the existence of large estates enabled landlords to abolish old customary tenure, demolish old settlements and build new farmsteads amongst replanned estates. The longhouses at West Whelpington (pp. 74–75) were deserted in about 1720, due to the policy of a landlord who realised greater rents from enclosing the land and erecting isolated farmsteads with more buildings including separate accommodation for cattle. Much of the

56. Cronkhill Farm, Attingham estate, Shropshire Note the farm office which overlooks the approach road. The farmstead was built for the breeding and fattening of cattle and has a fine range of looseboxes (illustrated) with thatch fitted under the slate roofs, a reflection of the widespread belief that cattle would fatten best in heated conditions. The Fifth Lord Berwick moved to Cronkhill soon after 1848 and was a keen and successful breeder of Hereford cattle.

nearby Wallington Hall estate was reorganised by the Blackett family. The former system of infield-outfield farming had ceased by the early eighteenth century: at Newbiggin an eighteenth-century farmhouse, now a farm building, consists of a single room entered from the cowhouse end and therefore rooted in the longhouse tradition. Bastle houses at Fairnley and Hartington

Hall were made into farmhouses in 1732 and about 1750. By the late eighteenth century, farm buildings were being built around yards which faced south or east to catch the sun, as at Prior Hall and Gallows Hill (fig. 1).

The early nineteenth century saw three local architects at work rebuilding farmsteads on the Duke of Northumberland's massive Alnwick Castle estate: David Stephenson was made estate architect in 1805. John Green, whose father made farm implements, built many farmsteads on both the Alnwick and Beaufront Castle estates, the latter including massive steadings built around 1824 with up to six fold-yards each. Such farmsteads, invariably of the E-type plan with wheel house and barn projecting outwards to the north of foldyards (see fig. 49), served a rapidly expanding population at the mouths of the Tyne, Wear and Tees. William Cobbett, writing in the 1820s, was amazed to see 'immense tracts of corn land', noting 'more than a hundred corn stacks in one yard'. 'The farmsteads', he observed, 'are, in fact, factories for making corn and meat, carried on principally by the means of horses and machinery'.

Farmsteads into the nineteenth century on these large estates in Northumberland and Durham were characterised by groups of farmworkers' cottages, products of a bondage system and a scattered rural population. Each labourer, called a hind, had to enter in bond with his employer by pledging his own work and that of a woman labourer: in return he was given a cottage, and usually a cash wage, a cow, fuel and a plot of land. In this area, the pressures on available labour due to the increasing demands of heavy industry upon available labour resources also led to the continued employment of women: in the south and east, women had ceased to perform heavy tasks such as ploughing, thatching and threshing after 1750.

Similar systems had prevailed on many medieval estates. A treatise of about 1200 (the 'Seneschaucie') stated that farmworkers were bound to sleep with their animals; they were sometimes provided separate rooms with fireplaces. Farm animals needed constant care and accommodation for farm labourers over stables or byres remained a popular feature of larger farms. On the Lleyn peninsula in north Wales, for example, each stable loft might accommodate up to eight servants until the 1950s. In Yorkshire, seventeenth-century inventories refer to farmworkers being accommodated in lofts over byres, stables or barns. At Low Hall, Appletreewick, the farmyard has two barns of 1691 which both have outside steps reaching lofted ends, one of these having a fine mullioned window. The lofts here and elsewhere in Yorkshire were commonly known as 'paddylofts' after the migrant Irish farmworkers who entered into contract to work on farms at the annual hiring fairs.

On many farms, labourers might be accommodated in the men's room over the back kitchen of the farmhouse. In Yorkshire's East Riding, up to twenty farmworkers could be accommodated in such barrack-like rooms. On the Attingham estate in Shropshire we find servants' accommodation provided from the late eighteenth century. Three cottages were built next to the farmhouse of about 1800 at Uckington, which employed ten men and two boys during the 1880 census. At Lower Betton, built in about 1780, the men's room was reached from a fixed ladder placed next to the kitchen fireplace. In 1880 each farm still accommodated an average of nearly four living-in workers. The large farmstead of about 1850 at Lower Brompton has iron bars separating male from female accommodation in the farmhouse.

8
The Industrial Farmstead

THE Victorian period, the age of the scientist and the engineer, still saw great landowners such as the Prince Consort and the Duke of Bedford in the forefront of agricultural change, and vast sums of money were spent on their model farms. £85,000 was spent on 39 new farms on Lord Bagot's Derbyshire estate between 1862 and 1893, and at least £700,000 on the Holkham estate in the nineteenth century. There were easier ways of investing one's money: 'funds pay punctual and the gates never want repairin' wrote Surtees. The Duke of Northumberland ploughed one million pounds into his estate but expected only a 2–5 per cent return – half that he could expect from commercial ventures. Land, however, conferred power and influence on its holders and farm buildings remained a symbol of landlord paternalism – and not without good reason, as tenants still usually voted according to their lords' wishes until the Liberal reforms of the 1880s.

Corn prices had risen in the 1830s but foreign imports soon followed the Repeal of the protectionist Corn Laws (heavy duties on import of corn) in 1846. The population of England and Wales had risen from 12 million in 1821 to 16 million in 1841 and 26 million in 1881, and in order to keep foreign competition at bay and meet this expanding home market – rising living standards made meat more expensive than grain in the 1850s – resources were directed to more intensive methods of production.

Mechanisation spread in southern England as labour costs rose from the 1850s. Between 1851 and 1871 250,000 agricultural workers left the land and by 1911 their numbers had been halved. Implement sheds with lockable doors – recommended by Tusser in the 1550s – were built on many farms from the 1850s. Large estates had their own smithies.

Government loans encouraged more drainage from the 1840s. Lime became cheaper and more available due to the expansion of coal mining and the railway network, and much arable land was rotated more frequently, which meant fewer root crops but more artificial fertilisers and stall-feeding of more cattle to produce manure. Superphosphates were marketed after 1843, and nitrates were imported from Chile and guano from Peru. Imports of guano had risen from 26,000 tons (26,208 tonnes) in 1841–3 to 165,350 tons (166,729 tonnes) in 1851–3. Fertiliser stores appeared on farm plans from the 1850s.

On advanced farms the use of hay and

57. *Coleshill Model Farm, Oxfordshire, 1853–4* (from *The Builder*, 1854). This farm was built by the architect George Lamb for the Earl of Radnor, and the layout was arranged by his agent George Moore. The rick yard was elevated 4 m (12 ft) above the other buildings, which enabled corn to be threshed, sacked and weighed in the first floor of the barn and roots to be thrown via a chute to the ground floor of the barn, which also received straw and chaff from the threshing machine above. In this room the chaff-cutter, turnip slicer and millstones for grinding grain were powered by a seven-horsepower portable steam-threshing machine outside. From here a tramway, with central turntable, took the fodder to a T-shaped cowhouse with cattle boxes for fattening cattle and skylights with louvred openings. The sloping site aided the drainage of fresh water from the upper yard and of liquid manure to the manure tank at the lower end. The barn was also flanked by a wool room and granary and the sheep-fattening house had a slatted floor with manure pits beneath. The buildings were fitted with sliding doors.

straw as standard fodder declined and more concentrated feedstuffs (such as linseed and rapeseed for oilcake from Russia and Persia) were fed to cattle. Some extreme observers even felt that the costs of erecting new stock sheds for cattle were met more through the increased value of the corn crop due to the production of dung rather than meat. G. A. Dean, in *The Land Steward*, 1851, wrote that a tenant would pay 10 per cent more rent for a 'compact and well-arranged steading' for 'it is there his livestock are sheltered and fed a great portion of the year, it is there the produce of his farm is manufactured and consumed, and it is there he collects the means of enriching his lands and of increasing the quantity and improving the quality of his crops'.

Increasing mechanization was reflected in the use of building materials. In the north and west Midlands, for example, agricultural equipment had been manufactured in Wolverhampton, and tile making concentrated in the Potteries since the early 1800s.

The removal of the brick tax in 1850 encouraged more building, particularly in machine-made brick; special types of bull-nosed and splayed bricks were made for doorways. Roof trusses, now usually made of imported Baltic fir, showed an increasing standardisation: the size of timbers for king-post roof trusses (fig. 24) was regulated by the Enclosure Commissioners for England and Wales from the 1850s. Iron nuts and bolts had been used since the seventeenth century, but Henry Strutt's farm

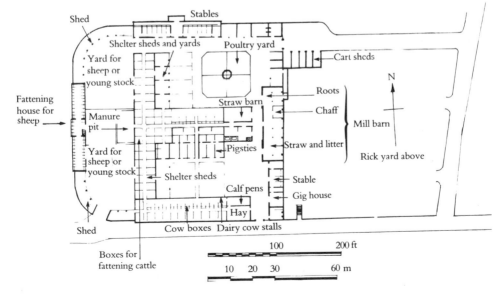

Shed

Stables

Shelter sheds and yards

Poultry yard

Cart sheds

Yard for sheep or young stock

N

Roots

Fattening house for sheep

Straw barn

Chaff

Mill barn

Manure pit

Straw and litter

Pigsties

Rick yard above

Yard for sheep or young stock

Shelter sheds

Stable

Gig house

Calf pens

Hay

Shed

Cow boxes Dairy cow stalls

Boxes for fattening cattle

100   200 ft

10   20   30   60 m

buildings at Belper, Derbyshire, built in the early nineteenth century to supply food to his textile workers, have iron roof trusses. Iron king-posts and struts became very common from this time (fig. 24). Staddle stones for granaries and ricks had been mass produced on Portland and the Isle of Wight since the eighteenth century, and by the 1850s cast-iron staddle stones, rick stands and columns for shelter sheds and granary floors were being made in Birmingham and other towns and exported by rail. Sliding doors, skylights with louvred ventilators for fattening sheds, and corrugated iron had appeared by the 1850s. The first agricultural building of mass concrete was built in 1869 on Robert Campbell's highly mechanised Buscot estate in Oxfordshire. Many farmsteads had new cartsheds and implement sheds built to store increasingly sophisticated machinery. A remarkably advanced farmstead, which looks more like a railway station than a farm and was built between 1858 and 1860 at East Harptree in Somerset (fig. 58), was fitted with an iron-framed roof covered with corrugated iron by William Wright of Bristol, cast-iron columns and other fittings by Musgrave Brothers of Belfast and Baltic pine flooring.

Steam had been used to power threshing machines on some farms from the 1790s (Trevithick's engine of 1812 for a Cornish farm can now be seen in the Science Museum, London), but the development of high-pressure steam engines between 1800 and 1830 made its use more applicable to large farmsteads. A twelve-horsepower steam engine, staffed by one man to feed and clean it, could now thresh out 15 tons (15.2 tonnes) of corn a day, compared to 5 tons (5.04 tonnes) by a two-horse machine and 0.2 tons (0.102 tonnes) by flail; it should be noted that the use of the flail, or 'poverty stick', continued to be encouraged on southern and East Anglian farms where surplus labour remained a problem until the 1850s. James Caird, in 1851, visited the extensive farm buildings of one of the Duke of Bedford's farms, powered by a six-horsepower steam engine, which cost £500 but saved £200 a year in labour costs. Each day, 200 bushels (7,000 l) of wheat could be threshed out for 8d per quarter, as against 2s 8d for the same task performed by horsepower and up to 4s if hand threshed. The shafts and belts transmitted power to the various cutting, slicing and crushing machines for fodder; steaming chambers, heated by the engine's boiler, could be used to steam roots, hay, chaff and potatoes and other roots could be boiled. Again, Caird noted that a 1,000 acre (400 hectare) farm in the East Riding powered 'every imaginable machine for converting the corn and vegetable produce of the farm into food for the sustenance of man and beast'. Barns on these farms became mills for processing fodder. A farm built in 1861 at Uphampton, Herefordshire, erected for Lord Bateman by Tuxford and Sons of Boston in Lincolnshire, had a twelve-horsepower steam engine which threshed the corn, taken by tramway to a covered shed north of the mill house, and processed the fodder. Once threshed, the straw was taken by elevator to be dropped down to the cattle below, and the grain was conveyed by auger to the granary.

Whereas the Meikle-type threshing machine could be repaired or even built by the village wright, the steam engine was strictly the province of the engineer, and, significantly, it was engineers as well as architects who designed Victorian farm buildings. Shaw Farm, Windsor, was designed in 1853 for the Prince Consort by G. A. Dean, who styled himself as land agent, architect and engineer, and designed many plain no-nonsense farm buildings in the 1850s and 1860s. He paid remarkable attention to detail. Egmere Farm, built on the Holkham estate in 1851–6, even has specially designed latches which prevented cattle nosing loosebox doors open. J. Bailey-Denton, an engineer to the General Land Drainage and Improvement Company – an organisation which forwarded loans for drainage and farm buildings – published in 1864 a book of farmstead plans with designs by engineers, including himself.

Industrialisation put advanced farmsteads in an excellent position to market their produce. Corn could now be steam threshed and exported by rail within a day. An observer of Hampshire agriculture in the 1850s noted that all the important farms were less than four miles from the nearest railway station, which took farm produce to the towns and brought artificial foods and fertiliser to the farm. Many of the farmsteads featured in Bailey-Denton's book were situated next to railways or large industrial centres – such as Toothill Farm designed by Denton himself and 1.5 miles (2.4 km) from Romsey Station in Hampshire, or the farm by William Wilkinson at Longleat Park, Wiltshire, which is 3 miles (4.8 km) from Weymouth Station.

Farmers experimented with many unusual layouts, which were too expensive to achieve any lasting popularity. The centrical farmstead was the most popular of these designs. James Tuke in 1800 drew plans for a circular cowhouse with central fodder room, Richard Lugar's piggery design of 1807 had sties and dung pits arranged around a steam cooker, and Samuel Wyatt, in about 1800, built an octagonal farmstead at Doddington Hall, Cheshire, with cow sheds radiating from a central barn. In 1884 Alfred Waterhouse, better known as architect of Manchester Town Hall and the Natural History Museum, included a circular cowhouse served by a narrow-gauge railway on a farmstead he designed at Buckhold in Berkshire.

Instead, the Victorian model farmstead became a steam-powered version of its Georgian predecessor. The barn, in its new role as a mill for processing food, retained its customary position between the rickyard and to the north of the other buildings, many examples now projecting into the rickyard (see fig. 57). Various methods maximised the production of food and manure from the farmstead. An increasing number of farms built liquid manure pits, advocated since John Evelyn in 1675, and the covered yard (see fig. 58). Work by Dr Augustus Voelcker and others proved that manure kept twice its value if cattle were left in covered yards with gutters: left in the open, straw and manure would be quickly soaked and diluted, and hence covered yards became more popular in damp climates than in dry areas such as East Anglia. Since at least the 1830s the Dudmaston estate in Shropshire had been buying large numbers of fatstock in September and fattening them over winter, and William Wolryche Whitmore was busily calculating how much oilcake and turnips each beast would need. Park Farm, which in 1832 had two straw engines and a turnip engine, was rebuilt in about 1850 – open and covered yards for fatstock were flanked by a hay barn and stable to the east, and a mill house powered by a steam engine with a boiler house to the north: a large fattening shed with sliding doors was added in about 1880. Other specialists advised the box-feeding of cattle which enabled the stockman to separate strong from weak cattle and meet their individual needs: from 1876 the cattle at Woburn Experimental Farm were accommodated in special boxes and regularly assessed on portions of weighed food.

Eastwood Manor Farm, at East Harptree in Somerset, was one of the earliest known farms to use covered

yards. William Taylor, a former butler who had inherited a fortune by marrying his employer's daughter, Lady Gourney, spent £15,000 on the buildings and lavished much expense on improving the lands of his 980 acre (392 hectare) farm. The buildings were designed by Taylor's agent, Robert Smith, who in the 1840s had designed farmsteads on Exmoor for the ironmaster Francis Wright. The main feature of the layout was the covered yards, an advantage noted by the local Post Office Directory of 1866: 'The great object to be attained by a covered homestead is to concentrate the farm offices and mechanical power under one roof ... [and] ... economy of time, labour, food, manure, warmth and especially even temperature for the comfort and progress of the animals'. The corn, stacked in the rick yard to the north, was conveyed by iron trackways to the mill barn. The threshing machine, and the chaff cutter and fodder-processing machinery on the first floor, were powered by an overshot water wheel: sacks of dressed corn were stored on the floors above the covered yards. Water was also conveyed in small iron pipes to the cattle, and rainwater ran down the hollow cast-iron columns which supported the roof to an underground water tank and thence pumped through two fountains into the cattle yards. A 3,000 gallon slurry tank lay beneath the yards. Flush toilets were also installed for the farm's 26 workers.

Iron trackways were used on large farms for carrying ricks from yard to threshing machine and for the speedy carriage of fodder between mill barn and cowhouse. Most remarkably, Robert 'Tertius' Campbell built a narrow-gauge railway around his 3,500 acre (1,400 hectare) estate at Buscot in Berkshire (now Oxfordshire) to collect sugar beet for his sugar and alcohol distillery built in 1869 for £100,000. His cattle were fed on sugar beet and housed on slatted floors. He built a mill for making oil cake, a gas works which supplied an artificial fertiliser works, and built a large corn mill next to the railway on which milk was sent to London. Another noteworthy industrial farmstead was built nearby at Coleshill (fig. 57).

One more example would demonstrate the lavish – if short-lived – use of technology on Victorian farmsteads. The Leighton Hall estate in Montgomeryshire was bought in 1849 by John Naylor, a wealthy Liverpool banker, who at once rebuilt the house, church and Home Farm for about £500,000. They were all lit by his own gas works and the massive complex of buildings, including two circular piggeries, at Home Farm had the latest gadgetry – such as barn doors that lifted on counterweights into the roof, and a turbine. A funicular railway took manure from Home Farm to a manure tank and animal rearing shed at the top of Moel y Mab (a spur of Long Mountain), whence copper pipes spread liquid manure over the fields below. Within 30 years the railway was disused.

Many farmers could not afford such paraphernalia – 'many new farmeries are erected and called model farms, but very few can be considered as proper examples to be copied from others', commented James Andrews in 1853. The making of portable and much cheaper cast-iron horse gear and portable steam threshing machines from the 1840s, however, brought the advan-

58. *Eastwood Manor Farm, East Harptree, Somerset, 1858.* The central gabled range, with its first-floor granary, is flanked by the covered yards with cart and implement sheds to the front. The outer wing to the left was built as stabling for 8 teams of horses; to the right as a range of pigsties flanked by a horses' and sheep hospital. Exterior view courtesy of the Royal Commission on Historical Monuments of England and Wales.

59a.   *Steam threshing at Wooley Barton Farm, Beaford, Devon, c. 1910*
Note the steam engine to the right of the picture, connected by flywheels and belt to the threshing box on the left. Portable steam-threshing machines could be hired out for threshing and could therefore be afforded by most farmers. They did not make rebuilding or replanning of the farmstead necessary but made many barns redundant because the corn could now be threshed, winnowed and sacked anywhere on the farm. Photograph courtesy of the Beaford Centre, Devon.

59b.   *Threshing by horsegear (below)*
Cast-iron horsegear also became very popular, especially on hill farms not easily accessible by steam engine. The horse stepped over the drive shaft, in contrast to the overhead mechanism in wheel houses which were rarely built after 1840. Courtesy of the Institute of Agricultural History and Museum of English Rural Life, University of Reading.

tages of steam to the ordinary farmer. A demonstration by the Newlyn Steam Threshing Company at Newlyn, Cornwall, was reported by the West Briton Newspaper in 1856: 'In the course of two days most of the farmers in the neighbourhoods witnessed its operations and were perfectly satisfied as to its capabilities'. Old threshing barns might contain straw and root cutters and other fodder-processing equipment, but it was now no longer necessary to store unthreshed corn in the barn because threshing could now be performed out in the fields. Thomas Hardy, in *Tess of the d'Urbervilles* (1891), described the portable steam-threshing machine as a 'red tyrant' worked by an engineer who 'spoke in a strange northern accent'.

In 1870, Clayton and Shuttleworth, one of several prospering engineering firms, employed 1,200 men to turn out 1,200 steam engines and 900 threshing machines, and by 1890 two-thirds of English corn was steam-threshed. Farms with steam-driven machinery remained most uncommon in areas with small hill farms, such as Devon and Wales, where wheel houses and cast-iron horse gear were used into recent times: wheel houses, not built in lowland areas after 1840, were still being built on the Rolle estate in north Devon in the 1880s.

Rising living standards amongst the industrial populace spurred the expansion of the fatstock and dairy industries. In 1878 James Caird wrote that 'Thirty years ago, probably not more than one-third of the people in this country consumed animal food more than once a week. Now, nearly all of them eat it, in meat or cheese or butter, once a week'. Consumption of milk in England had risen from 170 million gallons (646 million litres) in 1861 to 600 million gallons (2,280 million litres) in 1900.

Four-course turnip husbandry had always been difficult on clay soils, difficult to drain and stiff to plough. But from 1850 stability in the corn market and a 50 per cent rise in demand for meat and dairy produce prompted farmers in these areas to specialise in grassland husbandry, increasing fertility by the application of artificial manures such as bone dust.

In Cheshire, the numbers of cattle doubled between 1830 and 1860 and the fine farmsteads of the Wilbraham and Tollemache estates in south Cheshire bear witness to the prosperity of its dairy industry: since the late sixteenth century great quantities of Nantwich cheese had been exported to London. Brine Pits Farm near Nantwich had seen its cheese production per acre increase from 88 cwt in 1832 to 120 cwt in 1838, after its land had been drained and dressed with bone dust. Cheshire farmsteads had little provision for stabling and carts but grand Dutch barns built of brick for hay. Tall two-storey cowhouses with square and later round pitching holes to the hay lofts had been a feature of Cheshire and indeed many pastoral farms since the eighteenth century. Roots were grown purely as fodder crops and not in rotation with other crops. At Tattenhall Farm, corn and hay were stored in skeleton barns north of the root house, powered by a steam engine, whence food was carried by truck to about 80 dairy cattle. The cattle were fed on steamed food throughout the winter (mostly from 18–20 acres, or 7–8 hectares, of swedes and mangolds) and as spring approached oilcake, bean-meal and chopped seeds and clover were added.

Cornwall was another area which turned to pastoral farming after 1815, so avoiding the worst effects of the post-1880 depression. On the Cotehele estate in east Cornwall many eighteenth-century two-storey byre-barns had root houses and cowhouses added in the mid-nineteenth century. Haye Farm, for example, grew into the only court-

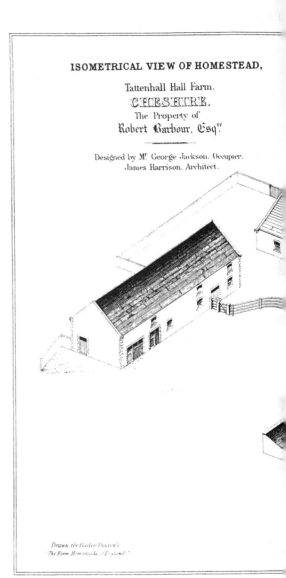

ISOMETRICAL VIEW OF HOMESTEAD,

Tattenhall Hall Farm,

CHESHIRE.

The Property of

Robert Barbour, Esq.

Designed by Mr George Jackson. Occupier.
James Harrison. Architect.

Drawn for Bailey Denton's "The Farm Homesteads of England."

yard farm on this estate: the fine late eighteenth-century two-storey bank barn had, in about 1850, root houses and fodder stores added to the sides which open onto cowhouses of the same date which flank the yard.

With the expansion of the railway network, dairy farmers were in a better position to export produce to the towns. Before this time, farmers had taken cans of liquid milk by ass or donk-

FARM HOMESTEADS OF ENGLAND.

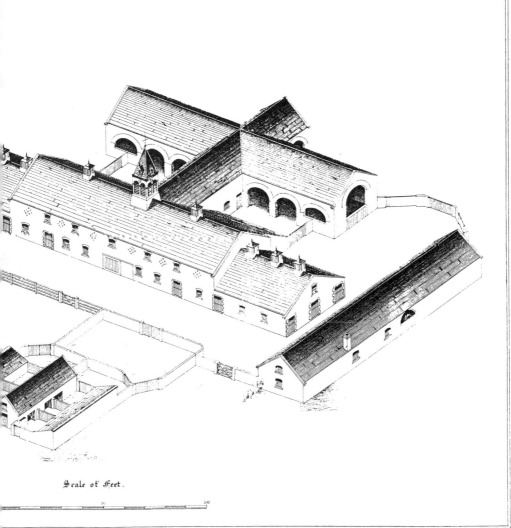

Scale of Feet.

C R CHEFFINS LITHC ABINGDON ST LONDON S.W

60. *Tattenhall Hall Farm* built by James Harrison (a designer of many Cheshire farmsteads) in about 1860. From J. Bailey Denton, *The Farm Homesteads of England*, 1863. See p. 132 for plan of Tattenhall Hall Farm, redrawn from J. Bailey Denton, *The Farm Homesteads of England*, 1863. It is for a dairy farmstead, in many ways conventional, with a fodder storage and processing to the north of the cowhouse range, but note that there are no yards for fattening cattle like at Coleshill (fig. 57). By the 1870s, however, much of the technological progress made in the high farming era was brought to a halt by an economic depression which lasted until the 1940s.

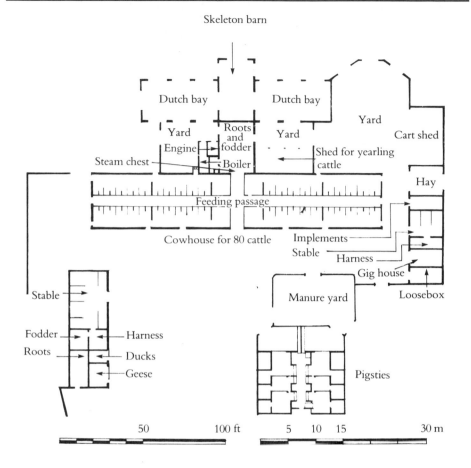

Skeleton barn

Dutch bay

Dutch bay

Yard

Yard

Roots and fodder

Yard

Cart shed

Engine

Steam chest

Boiler

Shed for yearling cattle

Hay

Feeding passage

Cowhouse for 80 cattle

Implements

Stable

Harness

Gig house

Stable

Manure yard

Loosebox

Fodder

Harness

Roots

Ducks

Geese

Pigsties

| 50 | 100 ft | 5 | 10 | 15 | 30 m |

ey to the nearest town (as John Farey noted around Uttoxeter, Staffordshire, and Ashbourne, Derbyshire, in 1817), or townsfolk had obtained milk from squalid and over-crowded urban cowhouses. Milk from the country was reaching London by rail from the 1840s, and imports increased to 6 million gallons (22.8 million litres) in 1867 – two years after cattle plague had wiped out stock in urban cowhouses and led to radical new guidelines for the more hygenic accommodation of urban cattle.

Sir Charles Edward Trevalyan, for example, converted many buildings to dairying on his Wallington Hall estate in Northumberland after the Northumberland Central Railway, of which he was chairman for eight years, was finished in 1872. He took the opportunity to sweep away wheelhouses, lay his estates over to grass and export liquid milk by rail to Newcastle, less than 30 miles (48 km) to the south-east. In prime dairy areas improvers such as Joseph Harding (1805–76) of Marksbury in Somerset had made farmhouse production increasingly mechanised and sophisticated. The first cheese factory in England opened in 1870 under American guidance, and thereafter the marketing of factory-made cheese put an end to many farmhouse dairies.

9
Depression, Tradition and Change

DESPITE the Repeal of the Corn Laws in 1846, 80 per cent of food was still grown at home in 1868. Soon, however, farmers were greatly affected by free trade, which brought cheaper food to the urban masses but led to a great increase in imports which eventually spelt ruin for many farmers. A string of bad harvests between 1875 and 1878 culminated in the worst harvest of the century in 1879. Corn from the American prairies flooded the English market, followed by canned and frozen meat from Australia and the Argentine. Prices, especially corn prices, fell and by 1939 70 per cent of food was imported.

Agriculture was now subject to the uncertainties of the world market: it had already seen its share of the national product fall from 40 per cent in the early nineteenth century to 10 per cent by 1880. As industrial wage rates rose, and land values and rents declined, farmers spent less on buildings – in the words of P. F. Robinson, writing at the end of another less severe depression in 1830, 'much expense may be saved by altering the old buildings instead of entirely removing them'. Buildings for cattle were the subject of most future investment schemes, such as those built on the Duke of Cleveland's Northampton-

shire estates in the 1880s or the magnificent dairy farmsteads built in the 1870s and 1880s by John Douglas for the Duke of Westminster's Eaton Hall estate in Cheshire. Many barns had lofts inserted and stalls and troughs built for the accommodation of cattle. New shelter sheds were built by Joseph Mawle, tenant of Cogges Manor Farm in Oxfordshire from 1877, who concentrated on cattle to the expense of arable but thereby prospered, unlike his neighbours.

The ensilage of mown grass to feed cattle in winter, which began in 1840s Germany, had obvious attractions to farmers in damp climates who found root crops difficult to cultivate and were largely dependent on good weather for haymaking. Air-tight concrete silos, built above or below ground, were known from the 1880s, often being fitted with hydraulic presses to consolidate the crop. Lord Armstrong, the rich arms manufacturer, experimented with silage on the Cragside estate in Northumberland, most notably on Low Trewhitt Farm from where he cleared away old thatch buildings. A silage barn, powered by a six-horsepower turbine engine, was added to the rear of the earlier threshing barn in about 1883: the turbine hydraulically raised and lowered tubs of silage into the silage pit – 11.6 m (38 ft) deep and concrete-lined – silage and roots were then taken by rail to a 60 m (197 ft) long fattening shed, and trucks on rails offloaded the fodder into bull boxes modelled after the type used at Coleshill. Armstrong's system, however, was only used for two seasons: lack of knowledge and scientific research precluded the proper use of silage until the 1930s.

Money and enthusiasm were no answer to farmers' problems. Vast sums of money had been spent on farm buildings, and with the Depression of the 1880s it must have seemed to many corn farmers who had religiously followed the pronouncements of Caird, Pusey and other disciples of High Farming that their model farms had been an expensive waste of time.

Indeed, rents had risen highest in pastoral areas since the 1850s and their many small farmers continued to specialise in pigs, poultry, dairy goods and cattle breeding: their farms, although small, were in the best position to shoulder the worst effects of the post-1880 depression. The size of 80 per cent of farms in South Cardiganshire in the early 1900s was less than 80 acres (32 hectares) and the relatively small size (50–150 acres or 20–60 hectares) of Welsh farms was reflected in the persistence of the L or linear plan, because hill farmers did not employ sufficient labour outside the family or grow enough corn to make the building of courtyard farms with yards viable.

As late as about 1860, John Rees (in his *Hyfforddwr y Ffermwr*), recommended the layout of two rows of buildings facing a central muck heap, a type of plan that had died out in Staffordshire by about 1800 because this design did not allow for more buildings. Reporters to the Board of Agriculture around 1800 frequently noted that Welsh estates were poorer than their English counterparts and lacked the capital to effect large-scale improvements. On the Erdigg estate in Clwyd the rebuilding of farmsteads was financed by the amalgamation of farms and the demolition of redundant buildings.

Even in much of eastern lowland Wales, oat straw was the most popular fodder and mangers or troughs for roots (which were often stored in potato clamps of slatestone rubble covered with earth) were not installed until after the 1850s. The only true model farm on the 42,000 acre (16,800 hectare) Ysbty estate near Betws-y-Coed was built in about 1850; the linear plan with house attached to other buildings is found in examples from the seventeenth century and the only other farms built around yards are the result of centuries of growth, such as the large dairy farm at Plas Glasgwym which has a seventeenth-century barn and a dairy with churns powered by water wheel.

In 1805 Bailey and Culley noted that on Cumberland farms 'no great extent of farm offices are wanted', generally a small stable, barn and byre usually attached to the house: 'Fold-yards, surrounded by proper offices, with a shed for cattle, are very rare in most parts of the country'. In the Lake District and the Yorkshire Dales improved courtyard farms occur only on estate or gentry farms such as the Lowther Hall estates near Penwith or Greenwich Farm in Borrowdale, rebuilt for Greenwich Hospital in the late eighteenth century. Another area with small hill farms, Devon, has very few courtyard layouts; one example is Newlands Farm near Killerton, rebuilt in 1842.

Many tenants did not repair their farm buildings during the Depression for fear that a rent rise might follow. A Royal Commission report recorded in 1896 that hay lofts in Welsh cowhouses left 'very inadequate breathing space for stock', the same complaint being repeated in 1923. Many Victorian ad-

vances were shelved until more prosperous times: thus the slatted or perforated floors for livestock used at Coleshill did not become general until the 1960s, when labour costs had made the feeding of cattle in straw yards uneconomic. On small farms tools and practices of Biblical antiquity remained: sickles were used on Suffolk allotments, and flails made and used on stock farms growing little corn in Devon in the 1930s. In Carmarthenshire, many longhouses

61. *Ciliehwnt, Caerwedros, Cardiganshire*
These photographs, taken in 1898, show the farm before and after rebuilding around a courtyard. Note the thatched roofs and dry-stone walls of the old farmstead. Photograph courtesy of the National Museum of Wales (Welsh Folk Museum).

were of only one storey until rebuilt with an extra floor and separate entrances for humans and animals in the 1920s; some Dartmoor longhouses retained the single entry into the 1950s. In the Yorkshire Dales some cowshed doors retain their ring stones, placed there to ward off contagious abortion, and tales still circulate of Dorset cowhouses having been visited not by vets but by folk healers who reputedly cured sick cattle.

The rise in dairy farming led to the conversion of many barns into cowsheds and the decline of the feeding of fattening cattle in yards. Electricity, again from the 1930s, also freed the farmstead from its traditional dependence on a fixed power source as its numerous outlets enabled machinery to be moved anywhere around the farm. The milking machine releaser plant and government legislation changed the face of the cowhouse and dairy; concrete floors and walls aided cleansing and prevented fetid pools of urine collecting in old cobbled floors, and from the 1920s the dairy was attached to the cowhouse. Mass concrete, first used from the 1860s, was improved from 1911 by reinforcing with steel rods: this reinforced concrete did not become general until the 1950s. From this time, government advice (based on scientific research) and finance has greatly affected farm building design. There were still 300,000 working farm horses in 1950, but stables quickly emptied as tractors soon reigned supreme. On hill farms many old farmers continue to muck out byres with shovels in the old way, but their sons have found that tractors can muck out new cattle sheds far more quickly, rendering old byres obsolete. Most old cartsheds cannot accommodate tractors unless their floors are lowered, but can store machinery. Moreover, most of the new improvers are not landlords but owners of increasingly large farms staffed by fewer and fewer farmhands. Only 11 per cent of English and Welsh farms were owner-occupied in 1914, but by 1927 the figure had increased to 37 per cent: the combination of land duties and income tax (from 1910) and the first World War had led to the biggest transfer of landed wealth since the Norman Conquest, and this process has continued to the present day.

Thus our historic farm buildings, kept in mothballs during the Depression, are rapidly becoming obsolete because farmers now need buildings with more space and larger openings. Old barns can, however, be suited for inwintering livestock and the bulk storage of grain removed by pneumatic conveyor. Hill farmers still use field barns for wintering their livestock. As the number of farmsteads decreases year by year, many farm buildings are taken out of agricultural use and other options become available: alternative uses are fraught with problems but can be remarkably successful, such as converting Pennine field barns into overnight accommodation for walkers, turning barns into sports halls or community centres (most notably at Lains Barn, Wantage in Oxfordshire), housing (the most difficult and sometimes least desirable option) or industrial units.

The future, therefore, is not completely bleak, and certainly a greater awareness of our farm buildings, more enlightened attitudes shown by planning authorities and awareness of farmers' needs will ensure that many of our finest farm buildings will be enjoyed by future generations.

Appendix

Some Farm Buildings Open to the Public

It must be stressed that farms are private property and potential enthusiasts must respect that privacy. Opening times of farm buildings open to the public – which include medieval barns such as Great Coxwell and Middle Littleton and farm museums such as Shugborough Park, Staffordshire, Beamish, County Durham, Acton Scott, Shropshire and Cogges, Manor Farm, Oxfordshire – can be found listed in *The National Trust Handbook, The Visitor's Guide to Historic Houses and Gardens* and *Museums and Galleries in Great Britain and Ireland.*

National Trust Buildings

Avebury, Wiltshire. Late seventeenth-century Great Barn.

Ashleworth Tithe Barn, Gloucestershire. Early sixteenth century.

Baddesley Clinton, Warwickshire. Mid eighteenth-century barn.

Bredon Barn, Hereford and Worcestershire. Early fourteenth century.

Bruton Dovecote, Somerset. Sixteenth century.

Buckland Abbey, Devon. Eighteenth-century farm buildings and fifteenth-century barn.

Cotehele House, Cornwall. Late fifteenth-century barn and dovecote.

East Riddlesden Hall, Keighley, Yorkshire. Aisled barn, *c.* 1650.

Erdigg, near Wrexham, Clwyd. Eighteenth-century dovecote and other farm buildings.

Great Coxwell Tithe Barn, Oxfordshire, *c.* 1300.

Hawford Dovecote, Hereford and Worcester. Seventeenth century.

Kinwarton Dovecote, Warwickshire. Early fourteenth century.

Lacock, Wiltshire. Fourteenth-century barn, and barn (now museum) and malthouse built for Sir William Sharington in about 1540.

Middle Littleton Tithe Barn, Hereford and Worcester. Early fourteenth century.

Osterley Park, London. Late sixteenth-century buildings.

Packwood House, Wiltshire. Seventeenth-century bee boles.

Shugborough Park Farm, Staffordshire. Home farm built in 1805.

Stoke-sub-Hamdon, Somerset. Medieval farm buildings.

Wichenford Dovecote, Hereford and Worcester. Seventeenth century.

Willington Dovecote and Stables, Bedfordshire, *c.* 1540.

Wimpole Home Farm, Cambridgeshire. Model farm built in 1794.

English Heritage Buildings

Bradford-on-Avon Tithe Barn, Wiltshire. Early fourteenth century.

Hound Tor, Manaton, Devon. Ruins of thirteenth-century long houses.

Kenilworth Castle, Warwickshire. Late sixteenth-century stables.

Minster Lovell, Oxfordshire. Fifteenth-century dovecote.

Priors Hall Barn, Widdington, Essex. Aisled barn of *c.* 1400.

Museums with Traditional Farm Buildings

Acton Scott Working Farm Museum, near Church Stretton, Shropshire.

Avoncroft Museum of Buildings, Bromsgrove, Hereford and Worcester.

Chiltern Open Air Museum, Chalfont St Giles, Buckinghamshire.

Church Farm Museum, Skegness, Lincolnshire.

Hampshire Farm Museum, Botley, Hampshire.

Museum of Cider, Hereford.

Museum of Kent Rural Life, Sandling, Kent.

North of England Open Air Museum, Beamish, Durham.

Pennine Farm Museum, Ripponden, Calderdale, West Yorkshire.

Ryedale Folk Museum, Hutton-le-Hole, North Yorkshire.

Somerset Rural Life Museum, Glastonbury, Somerset (fifteenth-century barn).

Weald and Downland Open Air Museum, Singleton, West Sussex.

Welsh Folk Museum, St Fagans, Cardiff.

Whitbread Hop Farm, Beltring, Kent.

Other Buildings

Details can be obtained from local information centres. One of the most spectacular is undoubtedly The Grange Barn, Coggeshall, Essex, built between about 1140 and 1150 and rebuilt with a crown-post roof in the early fourteenth century. One of the oldest timber-framed buildings in the world, it has been restored and made open to the public after attempts to save it from demolition: for details of opening times telephone the Coggeshall Grange Barn Trust (0376–62226).

Bibliography

CHAPTER 1

Chevenix-Trench, J.: 'Fields and Farms in a Hilltop Village', *Records of Bucks*, Vol. 20 (1972).

Davies, E.: 'Hafod and Lluest', *Folk Life*, Vol. 23 (1983–4).

Davies, W.: *General View of the Agriculture of North Wales*, 1810.

Farmer, D. L.: 'Grain Yields on the Winchester Manors in the Later Middle Ages', *Economic History Review*, Vol. 30 (1977).

Gill, C.: (ed.) *Dartmoor: A New Study*, 1970.

Hoskins, W. G.: 'Harvest Fluctuations and English Economic History, 1420–1619', *Agricultural History Review*, Vol. 12 (1964).

Hoskins, W. G.: 'Harvest Fluctuations and English Economic History, 1620–1759', *Agricultural History Review*, Vol. 16 (1968).

Wordie, J. R.: 'The Chronology of English Enclosure, 1500–1914', *Economic History Review*, Vol. 36 (1983).

Worlidge, John: *Husbandry*, 1694.

tershire in the Fourteenth Century', *Vernacular Architecture*, Vol. 15 (1984).

Evans, G. E.: *Ask the Fellows who cut the Hay*, 1956.

Evans, G. E.: *The Farm and the Village*, 1969.

Gooch, William: *General View of the Agriculture of Cambridgeshire*, 1811.

Hennell, T.: *Change in the Farm*, 1934.

Markham, Gervase: *Cheap and Good Husbandry*, 1614.

Mascall, Leonard: *The Firste Booke of Cattell*, 1596.

Needham, S.: 'Helms, Hovels, Belfrys: More Evidence from Probate Inventories', *Vernacular Architecture*, Vol. 15 (1984).

Newman, P.: 'The Flail, the Harvest and Rural Life', *Folk Life*, Vol. 24, (1985–6).

Rees, A. D.: *Life in a Welsh Countryside*, 1950.

Spray, M.: 'Holly as a Fodder in England', *Agricultural History Review*, Vol. 29 (1981).

Rose, W.: *Good Neighbours*, 1942.

Tusser, Thomas: *Five Hundred Points of Good Husbandry*, 1557.

CHAPTER 2

Airs, M.: 'Hovels or Helms', *Vernacular Architecture*, Vol. 14 (1983).

Archaeological Survey of Merseyside: *Speke Hall Estate, 1066–1844*, 1980.

Crane, E.: *The Archaeology of Beekeeping*, 1983.

Dyer, C.: 'Evidence for Helms in Glouces-

CHAPTER 3

Granger, F.: 'James Jackson's Diary, 1650 to 1683', *Transactions of the Cumberland and Westmorland Antiquarian and Archaeological Society*, Vol. 21 (1921).

Hewett, C. A.: *English Historic Carpentry*, 1980.

Higgins, M. and Martin, J. D.: 'An early seventeenth-century cruck barn in Great Langdale', *Transactions of the Cumberland and Westmorland Antiquarian and Archaeological Society*, Vol. 86 (1986).

Lowe, R.: *A General View of the Agriculture of Nottinghamshire*, 1798.

Rigold, S. E.: 'Some major Kentish Timber Barns', *Archaeologia Cantiana*, Vol. 81 (1966).

Rose, W.: *The Village Carpenter*, 1937.

Roberts, D. L.: 'The Persistence of Archaic Framing Techniques in Lincolnshire', *Vernacular Architecture*, Vol. 6 (1975).

Roberts, J. H.: 'Five medieval barns in Hertfordshire', *Hertfordshire Archaeology*, Vol. 7 (1979).

Tyson, B.: 'Low Park Barn, Rydal', *Transactions of the Cumberland and Westmorland Antiquarian and Archaeological Society*, Vol. 79 (1979).

Tyson, B.: 'Some Traditional Buildings in the Troutbeck Valley', *Transactions of the Cumberland and Westmorland Antiquarian and Archaeological Society*, Vol. 82 (1982).

Worgan, G.: *A General View of the Agriculture of Cornwall*, 1811.

CHAPTER 4

Alcock, N. W. and Barley, M. W.: 'Medieval Roofs with Base-Crucks and Short Principles', *Antiquaries Journal*, Vol. 52 (1972).

Bridge, M. and Dunning, R. W.: 'The Abbey Barn, Glastonbury', *Proceedings of the Somerset Archaeological and Natural History Society*, Vol. 125 (1981).

Bond, C. J.: 'The estates of Evesham Abbey', *Vale of Evesham Historical Research Papers*, Vol. 4 (1973).

DuBoulay, F. R. H.: *The Lordship of Canterbury*, 1966.

Brandon, P. F.: 'Demesne Arable Farming in Coastal Sussex during the Later Middle Ages', *Agricultural History Review*, Vol. 19 (1971).

Brent, J. A.: 'Alciston Manor in the Later Middle Ages', *Sussex Archaeological Collections*, Vol. 106 (1968).

Drew, J. S.: 'Manorial Accounts of St Swithun's Priory, Winchester', *English Historical Review*, Vol. 79 (1947).

Donkin, R. A.: 'Cattle on the Estates of Medieval Cistercian Monasteries in England and Wales', *Economic History Review*, Vol. 15 (1962–3).

Fox, A.: 'A Monastic Homestead on Dean Moor, South Devon', *Medieval Archaeology*, Vol. 2 (1958).

Hilton, R. H.: *The Economic Development of some Leicestershire Estates*, 1947.

Hockey, Dom F.: *Beaulieu: King John's Abbey*, 1976.

Horn, W.: 'On the Origins of the Medieval Bay System', *Journal of the Society of Architectural Historians*, Vol. 17 (1958).

Horn, W.: 'The Great Barn of Cholsey, Berkshire', *Journal of the Society of Architectural Historians*, Vol. 22 (1963).

Horn, W. and Born, E.: *The Barns of the Abbey of Beaulieu and its Granges of Great Coxwell, and Beaulieu St Leonards*, 1965.

Horn, W. and Charles, F. W. B.: 'The Cruck-Built Barn of Middle Littleton, Worcestershire', *Journal of the Society of Architectural Historians*, Vol. 25 (1966).

Horn, W. and Born, E.: *The Plan of St Gall*, Vol. II, 1979.

Huggins, P. J.: 'Monastic Grange and Outer Close Excavations, Waltham Abbey, 1970–72', *Transactions of the Essex Archaeological Society*, Vol. 4 (1972).

Kershaw, I.: *Bolton Priory*, 1973.

Miller, E.: *The Abbey and Bishopric of Ely*, 1951.

Platt, C.: *The Monastic Grange in Medieval England*, 1969.

Platt, C.: *Medieval England*, 1978.

Rigold, S. E.: 'The Distribution of Aisled Timber Barns', *Vernacular Architecture*, Vol. 2 (1971).

Victoria County Histories: relevant volumes for Oxfordshire, Gloucestershire, Middlesex, and Somerset.

Williams, M.: *The South Wales Landscape*, 1975.

Willis, D. (ed.): 'The Estate Book of Henry de Bray', *Camden Society*, Vol. 27 (1916).

CHAPTER 5

Alcock, N. W.: 'Devonshire Farm-houses, Part II. Some Dartmoor Houses', *Report and Transactions of the Devonshire Association*, Vol. 101 (1969).

Beresford, G.: 'Three Deserted Medieval Settlements on Dartmoor', *Medieval Archaeology*, Vol. 23 (1979).

Beresford, M., Hurst, J. G.: *Deserted Medieval Villages*, 1971.

Danachair, C. O.: 'The Combined Byre-and-Dwelling in Ireland', *Folklife*, Vol. 2 (1964).

Dyer, C.: 'Warwickshire Farming 1349 – c. 1520', *Dugdale Society Occasional Papers*, Vol. 27 (1985).

Dyer, C.: 'English Peasant Buildings in the Later Middle Ages', *Medieval Archaeology*, Vol. 30 (1986).

Field, R. K.: 'Worcestershire peasant buildings, household goods and farming equipment in the late middle ages', *Medieval Archaeology*, Vol. 9 (1965).

Hare, J. N. 'Durrington: A Chalkland Village in the Later Middle Ages', *Wiltshire Archaeological Magazine*, Vol. 75 (1980).

Hurst, J. G. and Hurst, D. G.: 'Excavations at the deserted medieval village of Hangleton', *Sussex Archaeological Collections*, Vol. 102 (1964).

Jarrett, M. J. and Wrathmell, S.: 'Sixteenth- and Seventeenth-Century Farmsteads: West Whelpington, Northumberland', *Agricultural History Review*, Vol. 25 (1977).

Jones, S. R. and Smith, J. T.: 'The Houses of Breconshire', *Brycheiniog*, Vols. 9 to 13 (1963–9).

Jope, E. M. and Threlfall, R. I.: 'Excavation of a Medieval Settlement at Beere, North Tawton, Devon', *Medieval Archaeology*, Vol. 2 (1958).

King, E.: *Peterborough Abbey 1086–1310*, 1973.

Parkin, E. W.: 'Bridge Farm, Bridge', *Archaeologia Cantiana*, Vol. 79 (1964).

Pacey, A.: 'A Cruck-Framed House and Byre at Hyde, Cheshire', *Vernacular Architecture*, Vol. 2 (1971).

Smith, J. T.: 'The Evolution of the English Peasant House to the Late Seventeenth Century: the evidence of buildings', *Journal of the British Archaeological Association*, Vol. 33 (1970).

Wrathmell, S. 'The Vernacular Threshold of Northern Peasant Houses', *Vernacular Architecture*, Vol. 15 (1984).

Wright, S. M.: 'Barton Blount: Climatic or Economic Change?', *Medieval Archaeology*, Vol. 20 (1976).

CHAPTER 6

Alcock, N. W.: 'Devonshire Linhays: a Vernacular Tradition', *Report and Transactions of the Devonshire Association*, Vol. 95 (1963).

Barratt, D. M. (ed.): 'Ecclesiastical Terriers of Warwickshire Parishes', *Dugdale Society*, 1955.

Caffyn, L.: 'A Study of Farm Buildings in Selected Parishes of East Sussex', *Sussex Archaeological Collections*, Vol. 121 (1983).

Cronk, A.: 'Oasts in Kent and East Sussex', *Archaeologia Cantiana*, Vol. 94 (1978), and Vol. 95 (1979).

Fussell, G. E. (ed.): 'Robert Loder's Farm Accounts 1610–20', *Camden Society* (3rd ser.), Vol. 53 (1936).

Grundy, J. E.: 'Notes on the Relationship Between Climate and Cattle Housing', *Vernacular Architecture*, Vol. 1 (1970).

Hartley, M. and Ingilby, J.: *Life and Tradition in the Yorkshire Dales*, 1968.

Hartley, M. and Ingilby, J.: *Dales Memories*, 1986.

Hey, D.: *Yorkshire from A.D. 1000*, 1986.

Holmes, I.: 'The Agricultural Use of the Herefordshire House and its Outbuildings', *Vernacular Architecture*, Vol. 9 (1978).

Kerridge, E.: *The Farmers of Old England*, 1973.

Outhwaite, R. B.: 'Progress and Backwardness in English Agriculture, 1500–1650', *Economic History Review*, Vol. 39 (1986).

Pringle, A.: *General View of the Agriculture of Westmorland*, 1805.

Quinion, M.: *Cidermaking*, 1982.

Raistrick, A.: *Malham and Malham Moor*, 1947.

Royal Commission on Historical Monuments, *Shieldings and Bastles*, 1970.

Rural Economy in Yorkshire in 1641, *Surtees Society*, Vol. 33 (1857).

Ryder, P.: *Timber Framed Buildings in South Yorkshire*, 1980.

Thacker, D. M.: 'Country Cider', *Folk Life*, Vol. 6 (1968).

Thirsk, J.: 'Seventeenth Century Agriculture and Social Change', *Agricultural History Review*, Vol. 18 (1970).

Tuke, J.: *A General View of the Agriculture of the North Riding of Yorkshire*, 1794.

Walton, J.: *Homesteads of the Yorkshire Dales*, 1947.

Willan, T. S. and Crossley, E. W.: 'Three Seventeenth Century Yorkshire Surveys', *Yorkshire Archaeological Society Record Series*, Vol. 104 (1941).

CHAPTER 7

Bailey, J. and Culley, G.: *General View of the Agriculture of Cumberland*, 1805, *General View of the Agriculture of Northumberland*, 1805.

Chapman, V.: 'North Country Farms of the Moorland Fringe', in *Beamish One, The First Report of the North of England Open Air Museum Joint Committee*, 1978.

Farrant, S. P.: 'The Changing Structure of Land Ownership in the Lower Ouse Valley', *Sussex Archaeological Collections*, Vol. 116 (1978).

Fussell, G. E.: 'Norfolk Improvers: their Farms and Methods', *Norfolk Archaeology*, Vol. 33 (1962–5).

Garrett, Daniel: *Designs and Estimates of Farmhouses for the County of York etc*, 1747.

Hellen, J. A.: 'Agricultural Innovation and Detectable Landscape Margins: The Case of Wheelhouses in Northumberland', *Agricultural History Review*, Vol. 20 (1972).

Halfpenny, William: *Twelve Beautiful Designs for Farmhouses*, 1750.

Hutton, K.: 'The Distribution of Wheelhouses in the British Isles', *Agricultural History Review*, Vol. 24 (1976).

Lambton, L.: *Beastly Buildings*, 1985.

Loch, J.: *Improvements on the Estates of the Marquess of Stafford*, 1820.

Macdonald, S.: 'The Progress of the Early Threshing Machine', *Agricultural History Review*, Vol. 23 (1975).

Wade Martins, S.: *A Great Estate at Work*, 1980.

Messenger, P.: 'Lowther Farmstead Plans', *Transactions of the Cumberland and Westmorland Antiquarian and Archaeological Society*, Vol. 75 (1975).

Mingay, G. E.: *English Landed Society in the Eighteenth Century*, 1963.

Muskett, P.: 'The East Anglian Agrarian Riots of 1822', *Agricultural History Review*, Vol. 32 (1984).

Neave, V.: 'Living-In in the East Riding', *Vernacular Architecture*, Vol. 2 (1971).

du Prey, P. de la R.: 'John Soane, Philip Yorke and their Quest for Primitive Architecture', *National Trust Studies*, 1979.

Reed, M.: 'Enclosure in North Buckinghamshire, 1500–1750', *Agricultural History Review*, Vol. 32 (1984).

Reed, M.: 'Indoor Farm Service in Sussex', *Sussex Archaeological Collections*, Vol. 123 (1985).

Robinson, J. M.: *Georgian Model Farms*, 1983.

Strickland, H.: *A General View of the Agriculture of The East Riding of Yorkshire*, 1812.

Vancouver, C. *A General View of the Agriculture of Devon*, 1808.

Wyndham, H.: 'The Farming Activities of the Third Earl Spencer', *Northamptonshire Past and Present*, Vol. 3 (1960).

CHAPTERS 8 and 9

Barton, R. M. (ed.): *Life in Cornwall in the Late Nineteenth Century*, 1972.

Carey, A.: 'The Leighton Park Funicular Railway', *Llanfair Railway Journal*, no. 101 (1986).

Collins, E. J. T.: 'The Age of Machinery', in G. E. Mingay (ed.), *The Victorian Countryside*, 1981.

Course, E. and Moore, P.: 'Victorian Farm

Buildings in Hampshire', *Hampshire Field Club and Archaeological Society Proceedings*, Vol. 40 (1984).

Davies, C. Stella: 'The Agricultural History of Cheshire', *Chetham Society*, Vol. 10 (1960).

Dean, G. A.: *Essays on the Construction of Farm Buildings*, 1849.

Dodd, J. P.: 'Hampshire Agriculture in the mid-nineteenth Century', *Hampshire Field Club and Archaeological Society Proceedings*, Vol. 35 (1979).

Farey, John: *General View of the Agriculture of Derbyshire*, 1817.

Gray, J. R.: 'An Industrial Farm Estate in Berkshire', *Industrial Archaeology*, Vol. 8 (1971).

Jenkins, J.: 'Technological Improvement and Social Change in South Cardiganshire', *Agricultural History Review*, Vol. 13 (1965).

Jones, E. L.: 'The Changing Basis of English Agricultural Prosperity, 1853–73', *Agricultural History Review*, Vol. 10 (1963).

Macdonald, S.: 'Model Farms', in G. E. Mingay (ed.), *The Victorian Countryside*, 1981.

Mingay, G. E.: *Rural Life in Victorian England*, 1976.

Perry, P. J.: 'High Farming in Victorian Britain', *Agricultural History*, Vol. 50 (1976).

Thompson, F. M. L.: *English Landed Society in the Nineteenth Century*, 1962.

Thompson, F. M. L.: 'The Second Agricultural Revolution, 1815–1880', *Economic History Review*, Vol. 21 (1968).

Weller, J. B. (ed.): *Coleshill Model Farm – Past, Present and Future*, 1981.

FURTHER READING

Baker, A. R. H., Harley, J. B. (eds.): *Man Made the Land*, 1973.

Brigden, R.: *Victorian Farms*, 1986.

Briggs, M. S.: *The English Farmhouse*, 1953.

Brooksby, H.: 'The Houses of Radnorshire, Part VI: Farm Buildings', *Transactions of the Radnorshire Society*, (1973).

Brunskill, R. W.: *Illustrated Handbook of Vernacular Architecture*, 1970 (2nd edn, 1978).

Brunskill, R. W.: *Vernacular Architecture of the Lake Counties*, 1974.

Brunskill, R. W.: *Traditional Farm Buildings of Britain*, 1982.

Caird, James: *English Agriculture in 1850–1851*, 1852.

Carter, A. and Wade Martins, S.: *A Year in the Field: the Norfolk Historic Farm Buildings Project*, 1987.

Chambers J. D. and Mingay, G. E.: *The Agricultural Revolution, 1750–1880*, 1966.

Crump, W. B.: The Little Hill Farm (Calder Valley), *Halifax Antiquarian Society*, 1958.

Darley, G.: *The National Trust Book of the Farm*, 1981.

Defoe, D.: *A Tour Through the Whole Island of Great Britain*, 1724–6.

The Devon and Cornwall Record Society: *Devon Inventories of the Sixteenth and Seventeenth Centuries*, Vol. 11 (1966), and *A Calendar of Cornish Glebe Terriers, 1673–1735*, Vol. 19 (1974).

Foster, I. L. L. and Alcock, L. (eds.): *Culture and Environment*, 1963 (articles by J. T. Smith, I. C. Peate, P. Smith).

Fowler, P. (RCHM): *Farms in England*, 1983.

Gailey, A.: *Rural Houses of the North of Ireland*, 1984.

Harris, R. *Discovering Timber-Framed Buildings*, 1978.

Harrison, B. and Hutton, B.: *Vernacular Houses in North Yorkshire and Cleveland*, 1984.

Harvey, N.: *A History of Farm Buildings in England and Wales*, 1970 (2nd edn. 1984).

Harvey, N.: *The Industrial Archaeology of Farming in England and Wales*, 1980.

Hoskins, W. G. (ed.): *History from the Farm*, 1970.

Hughes, G.: *Barns of Rural Britain*, 1985.

Jenkins, J.: *The English Farm Waggon*, 1961.

Loudon, J. C.: *An Encyclopedia of Cottage, Villa and Farm Architecture*, 1836.

Marshall, William: *The Rural Economy of Norfolk*, 1787. Titles in same series, *Yorkshire*, 1788, *Gloucestershire*, 1789, *Midland Counties*, 1790, *Southern Counties*, 1798.

Martin, D. and Martin D.: *Historic Farm Buildings in Eastern Sussex, 1450–1750*, 1982.

Mercer, E.: *English Vernacular Houses*, 1975.

Peate, I. C.: *The Welsh House: A Study in Folk Culture*, 1944.

Peters, J. E. C.: *The Development of Farm Buildings in Western Lowland Staffordshire up to 1880*, 1969.

Peters, J. E. C.: *Discovering Traditional Farm Buildings*, 1981.

Rackham, O.: *The History of the Countryside*, 1986.

Seebohm, M.: *The Evolution of the English Farm*, 1927.

Smith, P.: *Houses of the Welsh Countryside*, 1975.

Stephens, H.. *The Book of the Farm*, 1854.

Taylor, C.: *Village and Farmstead*, 1983.

Thirsk, J. (ed.): *The Agrarian History of England and Wales*, Vols. 4 (1500–1640) and 5 (1640–1750), 1967–85.

Wade, J. (ed.): *Traditional Kent Buildings*, Nos. 1–5, (1980–1986).

Waistell, C.: *Designs for Agricultural Buildings*, 1827.

Weller, John: *History of the Farmstead*, 1982.

Wiliam, E.: 'Farm buildings in the Vale of Clwyd, 1550–1880', *Folk Life*, Vol. 11, (1973).

Wiliam, E.: *Traditional Farm Buildings in North-East Wales, 1550–1890*, 1981.

Wiliam, E.: *The Historical Farm Buildings of Wales*, 1986.

Woodforde, J.: *Farm Buildings*, 1985.